The Lessons Learned Handbook:
Practical Approaches to Learning from Experience

The Lessons Learned Handbook: Practical Approaches to Learning from Experience

NICK MILTON

Chandos Publishing
Oxford • Cambridge • New Delhi

Chandos Publishing
TBAC Business Centre
Avenue 4
Station Lane
Witney
Oxford OX28 4BN
UK
Tel: +44 (0) 1993 848726
Email: info@chandospublishing.com
www.chandospublishing.com

Chandos Publishing is an imprint of Woodhead Publishing Limited

Woodhead Publishing Limited
Abington Hall
Granta Park
Great Abington
Cambridge CB21 6AH
UK
www.woodheadpublishing.com

First published in 2010

ISBN:
978 1 84334 587 9

© Nick Milton, 2010

British Library Cataloguing-in-Publication Data.
A catalogue record for this book is available from the British Library.

All rights reserved. No part of this publication may be reproduced, stored in or introduced into a retrieval system, or transmitted, in any form, or by any means (electronic, mechanical, photocopying, recording or otherwise) without the prior written permission of the Publishers. This publication may not be lent, resold, hired out or otherwise disposed of by way of trade in any form of binding or cover other than that in which it is published without the prior consent of the Publishers. Any person who does any unauthorised act in relation to this publication may be liable to criminal prosecution and civil claims for damages.

The Publishers make no representation, express or implied, with regard to the accuracy of the information contained in this publication and cannot accept any legal responsibility or liability for any errors or omissions.

The material contained in this publication constitutes general guidelines only and does not represent to be advice on any particular matter. No reader or purchaser should act on the basis of material contained in this publication without first taking professional advice appropriate to their particular circumstances. All screenshots in this publication are the copyright of the website owner(s), unless indicated otherwise.

Typeset by Domex e-Data Pvt. Ltd.
Printed in the UK and USA.

Printed in the UK by 4edge Limited - www.4edge.co.uk

Contents

List of figures and tables		*ix*
Acknowledgements		*xi*
Preface		*xiii*
1	**Introduction – learning lessons**	**1**
	Learning as a basic instinct	1
	Learning in organisations	2
	Lessons learned systems in organisations	3
	How well do they work?	4
	The value of learning lessons	9
	Reference	11
2	**Elements of a lesson learning system**	**13**
	Lesson learning approaches in the 15th century	13
	What is a 'lesson learned'?	14
	The steps in learning a lesson	16
	Closing the learning loop	20
	Trial and error, or trial and success?	20
	Survey results	22
	References	25
3	**Lessons learned approaches**	**27**
	Formal collect systems	28
	Informal collect systems	29
	Formal connect systems	30
	Informal connect systems	30

	A blended approach	31
	Reference	32
4	**Principles of lesson identification**	**33**
	When to identify lessons?	33
	The principles of lesson identification	34
	Aiming for the 'quality lesson'	36
	Examples of poor lessons	37
	Stories and lessons	39
	Self-identification of lessons versus lesson identification processes	39
	The questioning process – the metaphor of the tree	41
	Roles and accountabilities in lesson identification	43
	Reference	45
5	**Processes of lessons identified**	**47**
	Post-project reviews or retrospects	47
	After action reviews	54
	Individual learning interviews	59
	Learning histories	63
	Evaluations and assessments	65
	Incident investigation	66
6	**Writing down the lessons**	**67**
	Each lesson stands alone	67
	The lesson needs to be easy to follow and well structured	68
	How much context?	70
	Who is the audience?	71
	Attachments	71
	Quality assurance and validation	71
	Lessons must lead to action	72
7	**Taking action**	**73**
	Will there always be an action?	73

	What sort of actions are needed?	75
	How do you decide the action?	79
	Who assigns the action?	80
	Escalating the action	81
	Closing lessons	82
8	**Process ownership and process update**	**83**
	Who owns the processes?	84
	Local vs company process owners	87
	The role of the process owner	87
	Engagement with the learning cycle	88
	Lessons workflow	89
	Validation and escalation	91
	Documenting processes	92
9	**Ensuring lessons and updated processes are re-applied**	**95**
	Broadcasting new lessons and process improvements	95
	Process improvements and training	97
	Process review as part of operations	98
10	**Technology to support lesson learning**	**103**
	Lesson repositories	103
	Knowledge libraries	111
	Publish and search technology	115
	Tagging	116
	References	116
11	**Sharing and seeking the unwritten lessons**	**117**
	Communities of practice	118
	Peer assist	124
	Baton passing	125
	Knowledge handover	126
	Promoting conversation	128

12	The governance of lesson learning	129
	A governance framework	130
	Make corporate expectations clear	132
	Lesson learning systems	135
	Monitoring and measurement	135
	The supporting organisation	138
	Reference	139
13	The principles and processes of safety investigations *Johnny Martin*	141
	What happened and why?	142
	The investigation process	143
	The final report	155
14	Learning lessons in networks at Mars, Inc, *Linda Davies*	159
	Learn from where we are	160
	Learn from what we know	162
	Learn from the past six months	163
	Formalising the learning	164
	Summary	164
15	Wikis as part of a learning system; a conversation with Peter Kemper	167
16	How not to learn lessons	175
17	Conclusions	185
Index		187

List of figures and tables

Figures

1.1	Organisations with a lessons learned process (%)	3
1.2	Satisfaction with lessons learned processes (%)	8
1.3	The learning curve for improved performance over a series of repeat activities or projects following learning	9
1.4	Learning curves showing how learning can be accelerated	10
2.1	The learning loop	16
2.2	The graveyard of lessons learned	18
2.3	Learning enablers used by survey respondents in their lessons learned programmes (number of votes)	23
3.1	The four quadrants of learning approaches	28
5.1	After action review structure	56
7.1	Local and company learning loops	82
8.1	Shifting patterns of process ownerhsip	87
8.2	Example lesson flow	90
10.1	Technology and the learning loop	104
10.2	Typical format for a lesson database entry form	106
10.3	Example of a completed lesson	107
12.1	Governance framework	132
12.2	Chains of accountability in an organisation	134

Tables

1.1 The parts of a business that host lessons learned systems   4

1.2 The main barriers or problem areas that need to be overcome to improve the lessons learned process for respondents that scored 2 or less out of 5   8

Acknowledgements

I would like to acknowledge the input provided to this book by Phil Ridout, who critiqued the technology section; Johnny Martin and Linda Davies, who wrote chapters 13 and 14; Peter Kemper, whom I interviewed in Chapter 15; and Tom Young, who proofread the entire book.

Preface

This book is part of the 'Chandos Knowledge Management' series. It deals with one specific component of knowledge management – 'lessons learned'.

The phrase 'lessons learned' is common, yet people struggle to develop effective lessons learned approaches. The book is written for the project manager, quality manager or senior manager trying to put in place a new system for learning from experience, or to improve the system they have. It is based on experience of successful and unsuccessful systems, and recognises the need to convert learning into action. For this to happen, there needs to be a series of key steps, and this book aims to guide the reader through them. If all the steps are in place, and operating well, then 'lessons learned' can give huge performance benefits to an organisation. However, the workflow chain can be blocked, corrupted or broken at any stage, and little or no value will then be delivered.

The aim of the book is to provide a complete set of practical guidance to learning from experience, illustrated with case histories from the author and contributors from industry.

Introduction – learning lessons

Learning as a basic instinct

Learning from experience is the most basic of human activities. We all do it – even babies do it. They learn to smile. Through experimentation, through trial and error, and through trial and success, they learn that by manipulating certain muscles in their face, they can get a response from Mum and Dad. A little later, they find further muscle combinations that create sounds that obtain an even greater reward – 'Baby's first word'.

Babies are little learning machines, and grow up to be big learning machines. Stimuli and responses from the outside world are acquired, connected via neural pathways to existing mental models held in memory, compared against those models, and the mental models updated over time.

As a child grows older, she moves from unconscious learning to conscious learning. She decides there is something she wants to learn, and sets out to learn it. Maybe she wants to whistle, skip or climb trees. She may ask her friends, she may ask her parents, or her parents may take the initiative in teaching her something important, such as road sense, or reading. This is when learning first starts to become a problem. Have you tried to teach a toddler that throwing a tantrum in Tesco would be a bad idea? Or that putting biscuits into the CD player won't deliver anything of value? You are trying to help the toddler learn from your experience, rather than from his experience, and he doesn't want to cooperate. He has got on very well, thank you, learning from his own experience, and he wants to try a tantrum and see what happens. He wants to put a biscuit in the CD player and see what happens. He doesn't want to learn from you, he wants to learn from experience.

It is easy to learn from experience, if the experiences are powerful enough. You only have to put your fingers in the toaster once, to know that it is a bad idea. It is a lot more challenging, but a lot more beneficial, to learn from the experiences of others. If the experiences are bad, we would rather not learn the hard way by experiencing them ourselves, and as parents, we don't want our toddlers to learn lessons the hard way. We would rather pass on lessons, for the sake of all concerned. We would rather warn them in advance about the toaster.

Learning in organisations

If learning is such a natural activity, why is it so difficult for organisations to learn? If babies and toddlers can learn, why can't companies?

Perhaps we ought to ask, can an organisation really learn? Is learning something that organisations can do? Wikipedia tells us that learning is 'one of the most important mental functions of humans, animals and artificial cognitive systems', but organisations aren't humans, they aren't animals, and they aren't artificial cognitive systems. Unlike animals, organisations have no brains, so do they actually have anything to learn with? Does an organisation have a memory, or mental models that they can update based on stimuli and responses?

One company I have been working with believes that the route to organisational learning lies solely in having skilled and educated staff. They have mapped out the competences of their staff and identified the gaps, and their strategy to fill the gaps is to hire skilled staff, and to set up a programme of training for the staff they have, in order to close the gap. For this company, organisational learning is delivered through staff training.

However, many people recognise that organisations can learn above and beyond the sum of individual 'learning people'. Teams can learn, communities can learn, disciplines and projects can learn, just as an individual can learn. They can learn from experience, whether this is their own experience, or experience from other teams, other communities, or other functions and disciplines. It is this vision of 'learning from experience' that has led so many companies to set up a lessons learned process, so that if something does not go according to plan, they hope the company as a whole can reflect on what has happened, draw lessons from the past, and vow not to repeat them in future.

However, we will find in this book that lesson learning in organisations is far more complex than it is for a baby or a toddler. An organisation is not a single or connected brain. There are no sensory neurons carrying messages of stimulus and response to the memory centres. An organisation does not contain connected learning pathways, unless we deliberately introduce them.

Lessons learned systems in organisations

Let us start by asking how common lesson-learning attempts are in organisations. Do the majority of organisations have a lesson-learning system? Certainly most of the organisations that I work with have tried to put some system for lesson learning in place for at least some of their activity. This is particularly true of the private sector; there are still some government departments and other public sector bodies which have no lessons learned approach, but almost all of the private sector organisations for which I consult have made some attempt to ensure that lessons are learned.

To see whether my experience was representative, I commissioned a survey of lessons learned processes and systems when I started writing this book. Of the 70 people who replied to the survey, 76 per cent said that their organisation has a lessons learned system in place in at least one major part of their activity (Figure 1.1). A further 7 per cent were in the process of introducing one, 6 per cent had previously had a lessons learned system, but had abandoned it, while 11 per cent had no system.

Figure 1.1 Organisations with a lessons learned process (%)

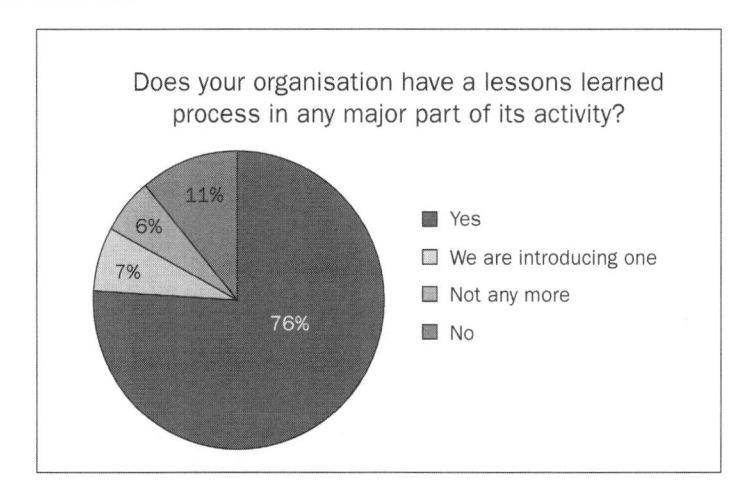

Does your organisation have a lessons learned process in any major part of its activity?

- Yes — 76%
- We are introducing one — 7%
- Not any more — 6%
- No — 11%

Table 1.1 The parts of a business that host lessons learned systems

Part of business	No. of organisations
Project management	24
All activity	7
Software deployment and release	4
Bidding and pitching	3
Industrial safety	3
R&D	2
Operations	2
Other	11

Within the organisations in this sample, lessons learned systems or approaches are widespread: they are in place or in progress in more than 80 per cent of organisations. The urge to learn therefore seems common.

I also asked which part of the business hosts these lessons learned systems. Responses are shown in Table 1.1, showing that lesson learning has been attempted as part of project management, bidding, software development, safety, operations and research and development (R&D).

So it seems common for organisations to attempt to learn lessons, and it seems as though there is a wide number of applications of lesson learning. But how well does lesson learning work?

How well do they work?

Even though the majority of people who responded to my survey have a system or an approach for learning lessons in their organisations, I also know from experience that these systems do not always work well. Case studies 1.1 and 1.2 illustrate this. These are drawn from in-depth learning assessments, and include quotes from staff interviewed within the companies. In the first case, a lessons learned system was theoretically in place, but was hardly applied at all. In the second case the system was more centralised and incentivised, but the difficulties in accessing lessons and concerns over lesson quality meant that the lessons were seldom reused. Neither of these systems were delivering the routine and systematic performance improvements that could have been possible.

Case Study 1.1 An engineering company

One of the few mandated global processes within this company is the project management framework, which is applied across the entire organisation. A core component of this framework is claimed to be the exchange of best practice and lessons learned. However, interviews showed that the lessons learned component of this process had very little rigour.

The first problem was that many of the interviewees did not know who was accountable for ensuring that lessons are identified and documented. It was assumed that accountability for learning lessons within the project management framework lay with the project manager, but this was neither made explicit nor documented:

> Nobody is explicitly accountable for this. The project manager is supposed to do it, but would anybody know if they didn't'?

Within the project management framework, lessons learned were identified in an inconsistent, informal and fragmented manner. One interviewee estimated that only 30 per cent of projects would identify lessons. The identification process varied from project to project. Some held fairly free-format meetings of the project team to discuss lesson learning. Others designated an individual to write an end of project review paper:

> What to apply and how to apply it is at the discretion of the individual project.

Once lessons learned had been identified, there was no single place to put them. Details were filed in project files, placed in the project intranet site, or included in project reports. Three separate lessons learned databases were identified in the organisation. However, the organisation had no effective search functionality, and it was extremely difficult to find lessons learned unless you knew in advance that they were there:

> Faithfully conducting the learning and then putting the results somewhere on the intranet will satisfy the auditors, but doesn't achieve much.

There was no defined process for using the identified lessons to update best practice documentation, procedures and standards. As a result, the lessons were identified, but then lost in the system, and the most effective way to learn from the past was to find somebody with a good memory:

> If anyone wants to know anything about lessons learned, they phone me.

Case Study 1.2 A manufacturing organisation

This global organisation operated a shared learning system, to exchange lessons and good practice on engineering and manufacturing. Lessons learned were identified by managers and specialists, and submitted to a single central system. A process for identifying lessons learned was built into post-project reviews, though these were often performance reviews rather than learning reviews. There was no similar process for identifying lessons learned embedded into the operational framework, so submission of operational lessons was ad hoc:

> We need catalysts for learning – it needs to be given legitimacy and priority, people need time to do it.
>
> Our reliance on people is a weakness because we don't systematise lesson identification.

> The central system for storing lessons was a database which could be accessed via the company portal. Lessons were often submitted in PowerPoint format. Initially the database was maintained by a full-time resource, which was later withdrawn.
>
> There were issues related to the quality of lessons. Use of the system was incentivised by giving each manufacturing plant a target for the number of submitted lessons. This resulted in a rush of submissions shortly before the deadline, which were often of very poor quality:
>
> > **People release lessons strategically, rather than when they come up, so they do not harm their standing in the company awards.**
>
> Despite the large amount of material on the portal, it was reported to be poorly used, because of bandwidth and quality issues. Also, although the submission of lessons was incentivised, there were no incentives for reuse:
>
> > **If you ask the project managers, have you looked in the portal, 90 percent will say 'No'.**
> >
> > **I could never log on to the global portal, and gave up.**

These are two examples of learning systems that fail to deliver the value that they could, but are these two examples typical? Again, I asked the survey participants. One question I asked was 'How effective is (or was) your organisational lessons learned process in delivering performance improvement? (if you run multiple processes, please choose the most effective)'. I requested that respondents score them between 0 and 5 (equivalent to a six-point spread), and the results are shown in Figure 1.2.

So it seems that staff in a large percentage of organisations are less than fully satisfied with the effectiveness of their lessons learned approach. We need to investigate more deeply why they are dissatisfied, and what was missing from their learning approaches. Table 1.2 contains a summary of the answers to this question, drawn from the survey.

Figure 1.2 Satisfaction with lessons learned processes (%)

How effective is (or was) your organisational lessons learned process in delivering performance improvement? (if you run multiple processes, please choose the most effective)

- Not at all effective: 7%
- Slightly effective: 6%
- Moderately effective: 6%
- Good: 48%
- Very good: 15%
- Excellent: 18%

Table 1.2 The main barriers or problem areas that need to be overcome to improve the lessons learned process for respondents that scored 2 or less out of 5

Barrier or problem	No. of organisations
Lack of follow-through and application	15
Senior management	11
Culture	10
Time issues	4
Other	11

There are several themes here; 'lack of follow-through' was the most prominent and mirrors the findings in the two case studies, where lessons were identified, but no actions resulted. 'Senior management', 'culture' and 'time issues' were also mentioned frequently, and may all be symptoms of the same issue – that lesson learning is not given any priority in the company. Senior managers do not promote or support it and it has not been embedded in the culture, therefore under time pressure it is loses ground to more urgent activity.

So it seems as if learning lessons is not so easy after all within organisations. Of the 80 per cent who attempt it, more than half are dissatisfied. So is it worth persevering? Is there value in attempting to learn from experience?

The value of learning lessons

The value in learning comes in avoiding repeating bad experiences like sticking your finger in a toaster, and in repeating successful experiences. If an organisation can draw lessons from experience, can eliminate repeat mistakes, and can reproduce success, then the result should be a continuous improvement in performance. This results in a learning curve (Figure 1.3).

In Figure 1.3 a learning curve shows the improved performance of a team or organisation over a series of repeat activities or projects, resulting from the accumulation of learning. Simply put – the more times you do an activity, the more you learn, and the better you get. The cost comes down; you do things better; you do things faster. The only factor you have at the bottom of the curve that you don't have at the top is learning; hence the name of the curve.

Most teams learn and get better naturally, over time, without any conscious focus on lessons learned. However, by focusing on learning, and by introducing a lessons learned system, their learning can be accelerated. This acceleration can happen in two ways, as shown in Figure 1.4.

If people in a team deliberately focus on learning from their own activity, they can accelerate, or steepen, their learning curve. This creates value, as they can reach lower costs or higher efficiencies faster than if they were learning naturally. In Figure 1.4, the difference between natural learning and accelerated learning is shown in the area in light grey. For example, people in one team that we worked with in Africa provide an

Figure 1.3 The learning curve for improved performance over a series of repeat activities or projects following learning

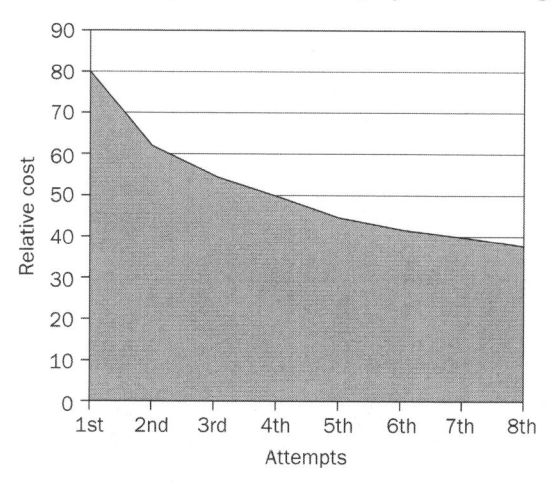

Figure 1.4 — Learning curves showing how learning can be accelerated

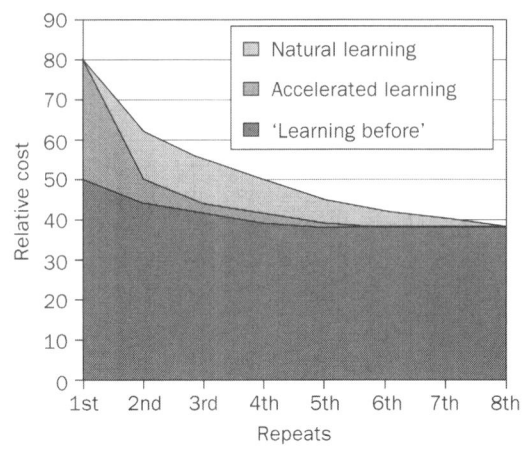

(Chart: Relative cost vs. Repeats (1st–8th), comparing Natural learning, Accelerated learning, and 'Learning before')

example of natural learning. They were repeating a task seven times. Through deliberate lessons identification and reuse, they managed to capture so much learning from the first iteration that they were able to cut the time for the task from 190 hours to 70 hours. Over the full cycle, this liberated about US$1 million worth of otherwise lost production.

If the team can acquire lessons from other teams, it can start the learning curve lower down. In an ideal situation, if all the learning already exists in other teams, then they can eliminate the learning curve entirely. For example, in the 1990s the Schiehallion Well Team in BP managed to eliminate its learning curve by doing most of its lesson learning in advance, by learning lessons from other teams, and thus was able to save in the region of US$83 million.

The value of this learning can be very high. A study on Shell in Oman found that by adequately managing lessons learned from past wells and applying them to subsequent wells Shell staff were able to drill wells in 60 days, as against the budget figure of 75 days – a 20 per cent reduction in time and cost against budget, and 40 per cent against the historical performance of 100 days (Ajimoko, 2007). That is a 40 per cent cost reduction, just through learning. Such performance improvements are commonly recorded in oil-well drilling, where performance is very tightly managed and learning curves are well documented. In other industry sectors, learning curves are not routinely produced, but there is no reason to expect that effective learning cannot produce similar performance improvements.

When we talk about learning curves above, we are talking about organisational learning curves, and demonstrating how the performance of projects or other activity can improve as lessons are put into practice. The same is true of individual learning curves. Individuals can learn to do their task more rapidly when there is a good lesson learning system in place that helps them avoid mistakes and reproduce successes.

So learning lessons is a natural human activity, one that babies and toddlers accomplish, which, if carried out within organisations, can deliver a very significant increase in performance. It is something the majority of organisations try to undertake, but at least half are not satisfied with the results, for a variety of common reasons. However, some organisations have succeeded. Some are very happy with their learning processes, and score them 4 out of 5, or 5 out of 5. Let us learn from these successes. We will look, in the next chapter, at some of the necessary components of a successful lesson-learning system, identified through the replies to my survey, and from experience over many years with lessons learned systems that really work.

Reference

Ajimoko, O. (2007) Technical limit thinking produces steep learning curve, *World Oil*, July.

2

Elements of a lesson learning system

Successful approaches to systematic lessons-learning have a long and illustrious history. The Golden Age of Navigation, for example, was also a golden age of deliberate learning. This was the 15th century when the premier learning organisation in the world, the Sagres School – the most advanced navigation study and research centre of the time, was in Portugal.

Lesson learning approaches in the 15th century

The 15th-century navigators were, literally, heading off into the unknown, and their lives, as well as their fortunes, were at serious risk. Knowledge – lessons from previous expeditions, from their mistakes and blind alleys, and from their successful voyages – was vital to them, and the navigators themselves realised that new knowledge and new lessons were one of the most valuable commodities they brought back. These lessons improved the chance of success for future voyages, and helped Portugal win the race for new territories and new riches.

Part of the eminence of Portugal in the navigation race was down to the learning system built by Henry the Navigator. Henry created the Sagres School – the most advanced navigation study and research centre of the time – where he gathered state of the art knowledge on astronomy, cartography and navigation. Before the captains set off on their journeys of discovery, they would visit the Sagres School, talk at length to the captains from previous voyages, understand their lessons and study their successes, study and copy the existing maps, train in the principles of navigation and map making, and read through the exploration journals from previous voyages (usually taking these journals with them, as reference). They would start with as full a cargo of learning as they could manage. Then, as they explored, they would capture their own lessons in the form of their own journals, and (most important) their own, new, maps. Gradually, voyage by voyage, the white spaces on the maps were filled in, and taken back to the Sagres School to build up the body of knowledge of navigating the new world. This knowledge was a hugely competitive advantage for Portugal, and jealously guarded from Spain and from England – the main competitors for new territory.

This was an effective learning system, where lessons were accumulated over time, encoded in maps and navigational guides, and transferred from one voyage to another. It had very high level support from the King of Portugal, and was treated as a matter of life, death and fortune by the navigators of the time. They were highly incentivised to learn. If they had a successful voyage, they returned with untold riches; if they had an unsuccessful voyage, they did not return at all. So the barriers we saw in the survey responses in Chapter 1 (lack of follow through and application, lack of leadership support, the wrong culture, and 'no time to learn') were not in evidence in 15th-century Portugal.

In this chapter we will investigate some of the success factors required to get lessons learned to work. We will initially look at some definitions and theory, and then use the survey results to validate and high-grade some success factors. First, some definitions.

What is a 'lesson learned'?

There is a lot of fuzziness about the topic of learning and lessons, and this can hamper the delivery of value through effective learning. If we ask the question 'What is a lesson learned', we can find very many definitions.

Here are a few definitions taken at random from the internet:

1. A lesson learned is knowledge or understanding gained by experience that has a significant impact for an organisation. The experience may be either positive or negative. Successes are also sources of lessons learned. Lessons learned systems tend to be more organisation-specific than alert systems (ESA, 1999).

2. A lesson learned documents the experience gained during a project. These lessons come from working with or solving real-world problems. Collecting and disseminating lessons learned helps to eliminate the occurrence of the same problems in future projects (VITA, n.d.).

3. A potential mode of failure (a risk) and the possible actions to mitigate that risk (Gerrard, 2007).

Elements of a lesson learning system

4. A lesson learned is an experience or outcome of a particular course of action – either positive or negative – that is important enough to be communicated to one's peers (AIRA, n.d.).

5. The knowledge acquired from an innovation or an adverse experience that causes a worker or an organisation to improve a process or activity to work safer, more efficiently, or with higher quality (BNL, 2008).

6. Knowledge derived from the reflection, analysis and conceptualisation of experience that has potential to improve future action.

We can conclude from these definitions that lessons are knowledge, they come from experience (positive and negative), and they can help or impact the work of others. But does that make them 'learned'?

Let us check them against the objective of lesson learning, which is to improve performance by improving the learning curve (as described in Chapter 1). Definition 6 above says a lesson 'has potential to improve future action' – but only mentions 'potential'. Definition 4 says a lesson 'is important enough to be communicated' – but communication doesn't result in performance increase. Definition 3 talks about 'possible' actions. We are going to need more than 'possible', 'potential' and 'communicate' if we are to deliver value.

I don't think these definitions are sufficient. Learning means changing your behaviour, or developing a new approach or a new skill. Learning implies change; not the potential for change, possible change, or communicating the potential for change, but actual change.

A lesson is not learned, until something changes as a result. The US Centre for Wildfire Lessons puts it: 'A lesson is truly learned when we modify our behavior to reflect what we now know' (Bailey, 2005). Lessons that sit in a lessons learned database or, even worse, in the back of a project report, are worthless, unless something changes as a result.

There is very valuable distinction to be made between lessons learned and lessons identified, which is made very clear in the lesson learning systems applied in the UK military sector. The operational units of the UK Ministry of Defence define an identified lesson as learning which has the potential to add value and which needs to be communicated, and a lesson learned as the change that results when an identified lesson has been acted on. I would suggest that many of the definitions above are of lessons identified rather than lessons learned. Look at the language in the definitions: 'collecting and disseminating lessons learned helps' – yes, disseminating may help, but what about applying them?; 'important enough to be communicated to one's peers' – what about 'important enough to be re-applied by one's peers'?

15

I would like to propose this definition:

> A lesson learned is a change in personal or organisational behaviour, as a result of learning from experience.

Ideally this will be a permanent, institutionalised change, but we know that lessons are not always permanent, and can be unlearned as well as learned, so I will leave the work 'institutionalised' out of the definition for the moment.

So learning a lesson involves a change in behaviour. Therefore a company learning a lesson requires a change in company behaviour. For this to happen, a whole series of steps are needed. These are the steps from identifying lessons to institutionalising the action. Let's look at them.

The steps in learning a lesson

There are three main steps in learning a lesson – identification, action and institutionalisation, which are outlined below and illustrated in Figure 2.1. Then in the following chapters we will explore best practices in getting these steps right, and doing them well.

Identifying lessons

The first step, identifying lessons from experience, is a process of reviewing, analysing and generalising.

Figure 2.1 The learning loop

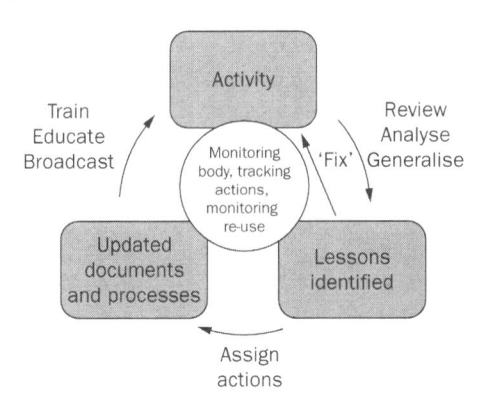

- Review experience. An individual or a team looks back on a project or event and recalls what happens. Activities or tasks are identified where there was a difference between what was planned or expected, and what actually happened. This can be a positive or negative difference – things may have gone better than expected, or worse than expected. These differences identify the learning points.
- Analyse the learning points. Here the individual or the team, often with the help of a facilitator, discusses the root causes behind what happened, and what can be learned as a result.
- Generalise for the future. What are the identified lessons? What should be done in any future activity to avoid the pitfall, or to repeat the success? At this stage we have a lesson identified.

The steps in the process outlined above are covered in detail in chapters 4, 5 and 6, where we discuss processes for lesson identification, quality assurance and validation of lessons, and documenting lessons.

We can describe a lesson identified as follows:

> A lesson identified is a recommendation, based on analysed experience (positive or negative), from which others can learn in order to improve their performance on a specific task or objective.

We are still not at a 'lesson learned' as there need to be two more steps in the process.

Assigning action

A lesson needs to be accompanied by an action if it is to be considered learned. If a lesson learned requires change, then an action will be needed, to make the change happen. I think this is a really important point, and it is a place where many lessons systems break down. All too often, lessons are identified, but no action follows. A lesson identified is not an end in itself, but a temporary step along the way to making a change, and to improving something. Lessons identified and stored are lessons that may never be looked at again, and changes that may never happen (Figure 2.2).

Think about an identified lesson coming out of a retrospect, or some other form of review. Have you learned:

- a way to do something for the first time
- a better way to do something

Figure 2.2 The graveyard of lessons learned

File your lessons here so we can keep on making the same mistakes

- a new way *not* to do something
- or that something needs to be fixed (such as equipment replaced, staff trained, reporting lines changed or a contract extended)?

The lesson points to one of several actions, such as to:

- document a process improvement – a better way (or a new way) to avoid mistakes
- document a new process
- fix something.

This list of possible actions is further expanded in Chapter 7, and examples of how actions are linked to lessons are given in case studies 2.1 and 13.1.

Case Study 2.1 Oil drilling

One drilling organisation in the oil sector identifies lessons by undertaking regular after action reviews (see Chapter 5). The drilling crew discuss their progress against the well plan, talk about what they have achieved, and identify things that have gone well and what has not gone well. They look at root causes, and identify

> the learning associated with those root causes. And then they go one step further – they identify an action to embed the lesson.
>
> Say they were experimenting with drilling mud, and found an additive which helped increase stability and stopped holes collapsing while drilling an unstable part of the section. The lesson is obvious – 'additive X should be used while drilling section Y'. The actions are also obvious – 'update the relevant part of the drilling guidelines' and 'order several sacks of additive X'.
>
> The drillers use a lessons database, which allows actions to be assigned; the actions are then tracked, and closed out when the action has been completed.

In the military, the action is often to update the doctrine (doctrine is the military word for standard operating procedure), and as somebody from the Ministry of Defence told me, 'a lesson is not learnt until doctrine is changed'. This is true where the action is a doctrine update, but a more general statement would be to say, 'a lesson is not learned until action is taken to institutionalise the learning', where institutionalisation means embedding the new learning in doctrine, procedure, structure, training or resourcing. Then if you can track whether the action has been completed, you can introduce metrics and a degree of governance to the learning process (see Chapter 12).

This step in the process is covered in detail in Chapter 7, where we cover the issues of deciding who takes the action, what to do if the action needs to be taken at a higher level, and who validates the action.

Implementing the change

Where the action is to 'fix something', then the lesson is learned when the action is complete. If the action were to 'buy a new photocopier for the project office', then as soon as that photocopier is in place, the lesson has been learned.

Where the action is to update or document a new process, procedure or doctrine, the lesson isn't learned quite yet. There needs to be a further step – to ensure the new process reaches the people who need it, and that they act on it. This step generally involves training, educating or broadcasting, for example:

- broadcasting the change in a newsletter or blog
- ensuring people are subscribed to an automatic feed for process updates
- incorporating the new process or doctrine in training
- ensuring people review process or doctrine as part of operations
- mailing the change to individuals accountable for reviewing it and implementing it locally.

This step in the process is covered in Chapter 9.

Closing the learning loop

If we make sure that actions are fed back into activity (either through immediately fixing things, or updating and then following new and improved processes and procedures), then the learning loop is closed, activity will improve, performance will increase, and we will travel down the learning curve. Much as a baby learns by updating their mental models, as new information reaches the memory through neural pathways, so an organisation learns by updating their processes and structures as new information reaches the 'organisational memory' through the organisational pathways of the learning loop.

In the example with which we opened this chapter, the 15th-century navigators, the learning loop was most definitely closed. Captains and their navigators captured their learning throughout their voyages, by keeping logs, creating new sketch maps, and recording the details of the coasts and lands they encountered. They brought these learning back to the Sagres School, the master maps were updated, and copies were taken on new voyages where they represented the most current updated navigational knowledge.

One important attribute of the 15th-century learning system, which is sometimes neglected in modern learning approaches, is that the navigators learned from their successes as well as their errors.

Trial and error, or trial and success?

The learning system of the 15th-century navigators involved learning from both failure (where not to anchor, which native peoples are likely to be hostile) and success (where to find fresh water, where to shelter in a storm, how to navigate out of sight of land).

Unfortunately, in many cases, modern learning systems seem to focus on failures alone. The lesson learning process is often triggered by disasters, accidents, ideas and solutions which have been rejected, or products which have gone wrong. Something goes wrong, the company brings its learning mechanism into play, and hopefully those mistakes will never be repeated. Chapter 13 describes in detail the processes involved in learning from accidents and safety incidents.

All of us – toddlers, babies, adults – learn much more powerfully from our mistakes as a result of the emotional charge and emotional and physical scars that failure brings. We only have to burn ourselves on a hot stove once, or be shocked by an electric fence once, and we have learned a lesson. This is learning by trial and error. This is what people mean when they say 'experience is the best teacher'. However, to learn only from failure has two negative consequences.

First, any company that learns only from mistakes, builds safe processes and products designed to avoid failure. You end up with band-aid processes, held together by protective measures. Now in some cases – areas of product safety or process safety for example – this is a good thing. In other areas, it may drive conservatism and risk avoidance. I would rather have processes designed to replicate success than processes designed to avoid failure. That is a subtle but important difference in outlook, and is the difference between risk management and risk avoidance.

Imagine a company with a health and safety learning and knowledge management system, focused on learning from mistakes, and triggered by safety incidents and accidents, and incidents of damage or risk to health. Imagine it has two identical operating plants, A and B. Plant A runs a very safe operation, and has had no safety incidents or near misses in a million man hours of operating. Plant B has a near miss once a quarter, and an accident every year. If the health and safety learning system is triggered only by incidents, it focuses only on Plant B. But Plant A is the one that knows 'how to run a safe operation'.

Second, if learning only analyses mistakes and failures, it becomes tarnished as a concept. People don't like it. It is a short step from 'let's learn from our failure' to 'let's hold a witch-hunt to see who messed up'. People start talking about post-mortems. The lesson identification exercise becomes a depressing experience, which it does not have to be.

The ideal for an organisation is that it learns from the minimum of mistakes, and from the maximum of successes. We know that it is human nature to learn best from mistakes, but we don't want to be at the mercy of human nature. Experience may be the best teacher, but it is also the most expensive teacher. We don't want mistakes if we can possibly avoid them, because mistakes can cost money, lives (in certain cases) and careers if they are big enough. Although a mistake is a powerful learning experience for a team, the ideal for an organisation is that *only one team* should have this powerful learning experience, and then other teams should not have to learn the hard way. The greatest and most valuable learning is to understand how to avoid mistakes, and how to succeed. Error must be minimised, so trial and error should also be minimised.

We cannot afford to let people learn from mistakes when mistakes are avoidable. The first time a mistake is made, it can be a mistake only in hindsight – at the time it might have been the best option based on the knowledge available at the time. It may have been a justifiable risk. The second time that the same mistake is made is a learning failure. The hindsight and lessons learned from the first mistake should provide the foresight to avoid the second.

An organisation should learn from its mistakes, *but only once!* The best approach is to learn once from mistakes, and many times from successes. In this book, when I talk about lessons learned, or learning lessons, I will be talking about learning from successes, as well as learning from failures or mistakes.

We have looked at the steps involved in the learning process and some of the components of the learning cycle. Let us check these against the results of the survey I carried out (see Chapter 1), to see whether the results we have discussed so far are reflected in the answers from my survey.

Survey results

As part of the survey I asked people to record which of several lesson learning enablers or components – the steps and enablers in the learning loop – they were applying as part of their lessons learned programmes. Figure 2.3 shows the results.

The most commonly applied enabler was the use of a defined process for identifying lessons from activity: 80 per cent of the respondents with a lessons learned system had such an identified process. The least commonly applied enabler was the use of rewards to incentivise lesson submission.

Some of the enablers that were identified as important in Chapter 1 – such as senior management support and sponsorship, actions associated with the lessons, and follow-through of those actions – are not used universally. If those enablers are important, then the companies that use

Elements of a lesson learning system

Figure 2.3 Learning enablers used by survey respondents in their lessons learned programmes (number of votes)

Enabler	Votes
A defined process for identifying lessons from activity	~48
A lessons learned database which can hold lessons from multiple projects or units	~37
Accountable person/people assigned to complete the actions	~31
Actions defined arising from the lessons	~30
A process for validating/agreeing the actions	~28
A clear accountability for identifying lessons from activity	~27
Quality assurance of this process (eg trained facilitation)	~26
Clear high level expectations from senior management that the lessons learned process will be applied	~24
A high level sponsor of the lessons learned process	~23
A method for disseminating the lessons	~22
A search function within the lesson database	~22
Quality control of the lessons to ensure they are well written	~21
An escalation method if the lesson or action needs to be addressed at a higher level	~20
A method to measure whether lessons have been captured	~19
A person or people to track the metrics	~17
A method to measure whether actions have been completed and lessons closed out	~15
Rewards to incentivise submission of lessons	~5

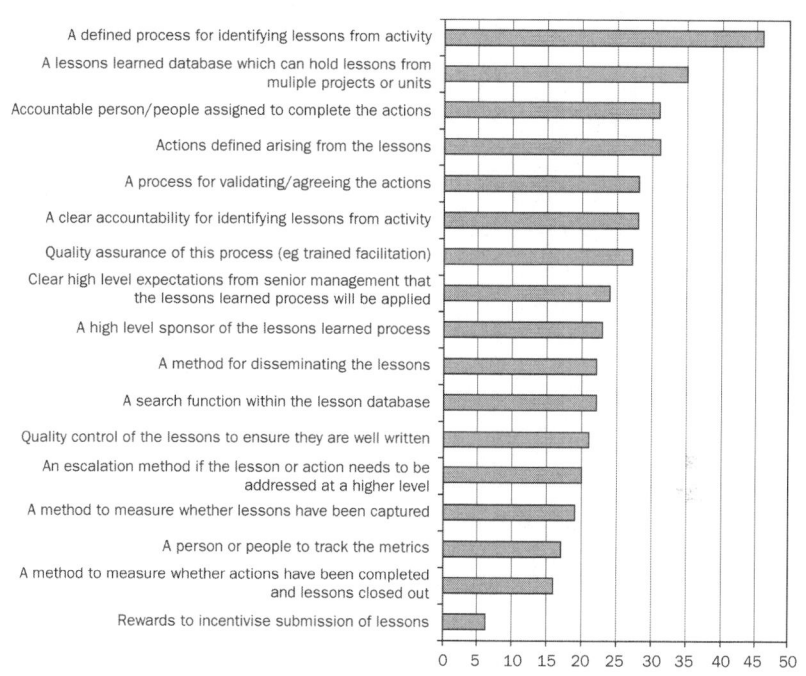

them should have better learning systems, and therefore higher satisfaction scores, than the companies that do not use them. We should be able to cross-check enablers against satisfaction scores, to see which of them improve satisfaction.

If we carry out this cross-check we find two things. First, the more of these enablers that were used by the organisation, the higher the score (in general terms), so most of these enablers are important in delivering successful learning. Second, the enablers fell into a number of groups depending on how much they affected the satisfaction score, as listed below.

Enablers that made a strong, positive contribution to the satisfaction score were:

- actions defined arising from the lessons
- clear high level expectations from senior management that the lessons learned process will be applied
- a method to measure whether actions have been completed and lessons closed out

23

- a process for validating or agreeing the actions
- accountable person or people being assigned to complete the actions
- a defined process for identifying lessons from activity.

Enablers that made a moderate positive contribution to the satisfaction score were:

- a person or people to track the metrics
- an escalation method if the lesson or action needs to be addressed at a higher level
- a clear accountability for identifying lessons from activity
- a high level sponsor of the lessons learned process
- quality assurance of this process (e.g. trained facilitation)
- a method for disseminating the lessons
- a lessons learned database, which can hold lessons from multiple projects or units.

Enablers that had a fairly neutral effect on the satisfaction score were:

- quality control of the lessons to ensure they are well written
- a method to measure whether lessons have been captured
- a search function within the lesson database.

Enablers that made a strong negative contribution to the satisfaction score were:

- rewards to incentivise submission of lessons.

The survey results seem to bear out the conclusion that lessons learned need to lead to action, given the strong correspondence between the satisfaction rating and those elements related to action (in other words, those lessons learned systems that included assignment of actions, validating the actions, and closing out the actions scored higher on satisfaction levels than those that didn't).

The steps in the process of identifying lessons, assigning actions and carrying these through into action will be covered in the rest of this book. In chapters 4, 5 and 6 we look at the first step in the loop: lesson identification. We will look at examples of identification processes, how to facilitate them effectively, issues of quality control, and how to document lessons. In chapters 7, 8 and 9 we will look at how actions are assigned to lessons, how lessons can lead to process update, and how updated processes are carried through into action. Senior management expectation and monitoring and metrics are covered in Chapter 12 under governance, and lessons learned databases are discussed in Chapter 10.

However, before we dive into detail, we will look at some of the philosophical choices to be made in designing our learning system.

References

American Immunization Registry Association (n.d.) IIS Best Practices, *http://www.immregistries.org/know/best_practices.phtml*.

Bailey, M.T. (2005) Wildland Fire Related Vehicle Accidents: an emphasis on the ATV, *Scratchline*, issue 12, *http://www.wildfirelessons.net/documents/Scratchline_Issue12.pdf*.

Brookhaven National Laboratory (2008) BNL Lessons Learned Workshop, *http://www.bnl.gov/qmo/linkable_files/ppt/LL%20Talk%206-27-08.ppt*.

European Space Agency (1999) Alerts and Lessons Learned: an effective way to prevent failures and problems, workshop 29–30 September 1999, ESTEC, Noordwijk, The Netherlands, *http://conferences.esa.int/99c06/index.html*.

Gerrard, P. (2007), Using Lessons Learned to Challenge ERP Projects, EuroSTAR, *http://newsweaver.ie/qualtech/e_article000828180.cfm?x=bcVhM0T,b4V6Phvj,w*.

Virginia Information Technologies Agency (n.d.) What is a Lesson Learned?, *http://www.vita.virginia.gov/itTrain/pmDev/bpll/BPLL.CFM?Q=LL*.

Lessons learned approaches

In the previous chapter we looked at some of the essential elements of a lesson learning system. Before we start to look at the design of such systems, there are some fundamental philosophical choices to be made. These are often made implicitly, emotionally or through assumption, so it is worth taking time to analyse them intellectually, before starting work on our lesson learning system.

I am going to look at some of the philosophical choices under two headings:

- whether we will choose a formal system or an informal system
- whether we will focus on connecting people or on collecting lessons.

The choice between formal and informal systems is important. A formal system has defined roles, expectations, technology and workflows. The system operates within a defined framework or set of rules. An informal system, on the other hand, has few if any defined roles or expectations, and operates in an ad hoc manner. The choice between formal and informal systems learning approaches is often ideological. Either we feel that learning and knowledge are organic processes that will be killed by any degree of formality, or we feel that learning is far too important to be left to ad hoc informality and chance.

The system can also be driven through connect or collect systems. In other words, lessons can stay tacit and unwritten, or we can try to transfer knowledge through the use of recorded or written material. In a connect system, we look at building networks of people who seek and share knowledge through dialogue and conversation. In a collect system, the transfer of lessons requires them to be written down and stored, so others can find them and learn from them. Again, the choice between connect and collect systems is often ideological. People feel that knowledge is inherently a human property, which can only be transferred through human

Figure 3.1 The four quadrants of learning approaches

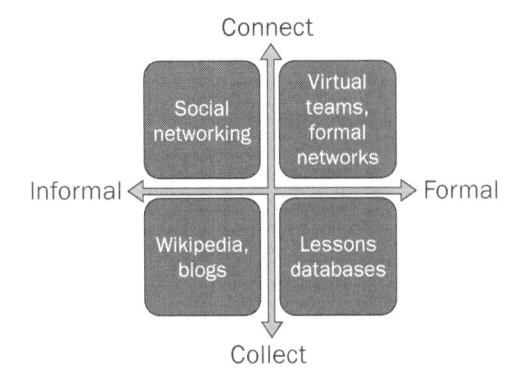

```
                    Connect
                       ▲
         ┌──────────┬──────────┐
         │  Social  │ Virtual  │
         │networking│  teams,  │
         │          │  formal  │
         │          │ networks │
Informal ├──────────┼──────────┤ Formal
◄────────│Wikipedia,│ Lessons  │────────►
         │  blogs   │databases │
         │          │          │
         └──────────┴──────────┘
                       ▼
                    Collect
```

interaction. Or people feel that there needs to be a centrally accessible knowledge base that they can refer to and rely on.

As Figure 3.1 shows, the interplay of connect–collect and formal–informal gives four quadrants, which can represent four distinct choices for a lesson learning system.

Formal collect systems

The formal collection (bottom right) quadrant is where a company has an organised and managed system for the collection of new lessons. This quadrant is the home of lessons databases. Examples of these come from the military sector, where sophisticated lessons databases form the technology hub for a rigorous and formal system of lesson identification, action assignment, and lesson tracking and reporting. Formal databases have the great advantage that they allow one to track, find, sort and group lessons and new knowledge easily. Each lesson is a single learning opportunity, and can be tracked to implementation. Other examples can be found in the systems operated by the oil sector (see Case Studies 2.1 and 10.1).

The issues of 'follow-through' (the biggest barrier identified in the survey reported in Chapter 2) can be addressed effectively with a formal collection system. Also the ability to track lessons, and to report statistics such as the total value of lessons, makes it easy to apply good governance. The formal Ford best practice replication system, which is described in Chapter 12, kept a running total of the financial value delivered through best practice replication. The disadvantages with such a system are that people find it frustrating or difficult to fill in forms.

In Chapter 15, Peter Kemper provides some strong arguments about the difficulty of what he calls 'transactional systems' and the challenge of allowing for creativity while still allowing consistency in lessons capture. It is more difficult to enter content in these formal lessons learned databases, though easier to retrieve and track content. Their natural home is in organisations, such as the military, where the consequences of failing to learn can lead to lost lives as well as massive lost financial value. Here learning is too important to remain informal. Industrial private sector companies may be open to prosecution on grounds of negligence if accidents recur through a lack of learning systems, and so may need a system formal enough to be able to prove that safety lessons have been distributed to all who need to see them.

Informal collect systems

At the other end of the formality scale (in the bottom left quadrant) are the voluntary, ad hoc and self-organising community tools such as Wikipedia. The Wikipedia model has sometimes been suggested as a model for sharing knowledge in a large organisation, allowing wisdom to emerge spontaneously from crowds. The great advantage of wiki technology is that it is extremely easy to enter basic content, and a little bit of technical skill allows you to add a richness of multimedia content as well. If you are motivated to publish, wikis such as Wikipedia offer a simple route, and the crowd can be expected to edit as well as to source material. However, there are drawbacks with the informal Wikipedia model. The 1:9:90 rule tells us that voluntary wikis draw on only about 2–3 per cent of available knowledge (as explained in Chapter 10), and all submissions in the Wikipedia model are voluntary and ad hoc. So unless there is a huge user base and massive redundancy or overlap in knowledge, there is a real risk that crucial lessons may never enter the system.

Also there is no guarantee that lessons, even if they do enter the system, will find their way to the user who needs them. With ad hoc entry and ad hoc retrieval, learning becomes a matter of chance. A Wikipedia approach may be ideal where learning is complex and tacit and needs creative expression, while the risk and cost associated with not learning is low enough that closing the learning loop can be left ad hoc. The approach described by Peter Kemper in Chapter 15 is a halfway house between formality and informality, using a wiki, but with a sufficient level of support and governance to ensure it will be populated with quality material.

Formal connect systems

Formal connect systems (in the top right quadrant) are the formal networks, expert locators and virtual teams, which allow members to use each other as a resource and repository of unwritten knowledge. Here lessons exchange is through dialogue, accomplished within a formal network of people or at a formal meeting (as discussed in Chapter 11). Anglo American, a global mining organisation, has run a system called Ask Anglo, where queries and requests for knowledge can be submitted online, and are then routed (based on topic) to the relevant company expert. In BP, formal networks are developed to steward knowledge and share lessons on topics of strategic importance to the company, each network having a budget, leader, sponsor and defined core team. Chapter 14 describes the formal structures and connections that go on within the global new markets community in Mars, which have delivered much value to the organisation through sharing and reusing lessons.

Formal connect systems are ideal for sharing lessons in areas of complex or context-specific need, for one-off requests, and for topics which are rapidly changing, and where new problems are frequently being identified. They are less appropriate where processes are becoming better defined and more standardised, and where lessons can be incorporated into standards and guidelines.

Informal connect systems

The fourth (top left) quadrant represents informal connect systems. Examples are the social networks found on the internet, such as LinkedIn and Facebook. Here is the extreme of informality, where discussion groups emerge from bottom-up interest, allowing questions to be asked, answers to be given and lessons to be exchanged in a loose and mobile network of contacts. The appeal of these systems is their extreme informality and ease of use, and the introduction of systems such as these can help to develop a more open discussion-oriented culture in an organisation. They also allow for serendipity – chance meetings with unusual sources of learning. The disadvantage is the great difficulty in ensuring that the right questions are asked in the first place, and then in making sure they are answered by someone with valid lessons and experience to offer. Many online discussions can end up as an exchange of opinions among a random group, rather than a learning experience: more gossip than an exchange of lessons. Such informal connect systems are ideal for beginning a culture change, but in my opinion do not support a systematic approach to knowledge sharing.

A blended approach

I firmly believe that both connect and collect systems are necessary. Any complete knowledge management or lessons learned system needs a blend of connect and collect systems, running both approaches in parallel. They need to be cross-linked, of course, and the communities or networks can be accountable for some of the collection, as well as the connection.

With the choice between informal and formal systems, the answer is to find the right balance: not a blend, but a balance. In any one company, for any one topic, to run formal and informal systems in parallel would confuse users, and often undermine one or other of the two: 'I know that is what it says in the official process, but what is the word on the street?' There is no value to anyone if the word on the street and the official line diverge. Which lessons will you follow in that case?

The balance between formal and informal systems on the connect side is found in the communities of practice, where a community will develop (or be given) a level of formality which suits their need and purpose.

On the collect side, Shell has arrived at a semi-formal wiki-based approach with an informal structure, with entry drawn from formal reports, and with the use of dedicated back-office support (Hendrix, 2007). Similarly the US Army, a long time user of formal push systems, is now experimenting with wikis as a way to build process documents, or 'doctrine'.

In this book, we are looking largely at systems and approaches towards the more formal end of the spectrum. I am assuming that you see too much value in lesson learning to leave it entirely to chance, and that you believe that some degree of systematisation and formalisation is necessary. Chapters 4 to 9 are concerned with collect systems, and Chapter 11 with connect systems. This disparity (six chapters on collect systems and just one on connect systems) reflects the complexity of the collect route, rather than its importance. This book recognises the importance of both approaches, but also recognises that the collect approach requires more attention, as there are more components that can go wrong.

Reference

Hendrix, D. (2007) Focusing on behaviors and learning at Shell, *Knowledge Management Review*, July/Aug.

4

Principles of lesson identification

The first step in the lessons learned workflow that we described in Chapter 2 is to identify the lessons. This needs to be done well and regularly, to cover success as well as failure, and to involve everyone who has valuable knowledge and learning to share, even if they don't realise it! You need to pay particular attention to the quality of the lessons, because the rest of the lessons learned cycle won't deliver value if the identified lessons are too poorly described to learn from.

In this chapter we look at principles and processes for lesson identification, when these should be applied and by whom, and the secrets of making these processes effective.

When to identify lessons?

There are two main approaches for choosing when to apply lesson identification: reactive and scheduled. The reactive approach requires someone to identify particular successes and failures from which to learn. The failures can be obvious, such as health and safety incidents or significant project overruns, and many companies have mandatory processes for reviewing these failures as described in Chapter 13. But how do you spot the successes? Maybe you can use your company benchmark metrics and pick the best performing units for review. Perhaps you could identify lessons from the manufacturing plant that never had an accident, as well as from the one with frequent accidents.

One organisation we have worked with uses its internal global consultants and technical directors to identify opportunities for lesson identification. They travel the world, reviewing activity at different centres, and identify good practice that needs to be captured, as well as opportunities to learn from mistakes.

An alternative approach, common within project-based organisations, is to schedule learning reviews within the activity framework. These reviews could be:

- after action reviews held daily during high-intensity learning
- after action reviews held after each significant task (for example, BP Drilling holds after action reviews after completing each section of an offshore oil well)
- retrospects (or some other form of post-project review) held at the end of each project stage, or at each project review gate
- retrospects (or some other form of review) held at the end of a project
- retrospects (or some other form of review) held within a set period of the end of the project; for example, the UK government holds a post implementation review a year after implementation of a policy, to assess whether it worked as expected, and what has been learned as a result
- retrospects (or some other form of review) held at the end of a bid process, when the company knows if the bid has been successful or unsuccessful.

There are many advantages to the scheduled approach. First, success and failure are components of every project, and if every project is reviewed, lessons may be identified from small mistakes, so that big mistakes can be avoided elsewhere. Second, if lesson identification is scheduled, it becomes a clear expectation, and the company can monitor whether the expectation is being met. This expectation (of scheduled learning within projects) is common in many organisations, though the rigour with which the expectation is met seems to vary. Lesson identification is supposed to be a component of PRINCE2, for example, but I still meet people in many organisations who seem to treat it as optional even though they preach that they adhere to PRINCE2. The chapter on governance (Chapter 12) covers some of these issues.

The principles of lesson identification

Before we get too far into the detail of processes for lesson identification, we need to cover a few principles.

Principles of lesson identification

First, just because we review activity, doesn't mean we are identifying lessons. Not every review is designed to identify lessons. There can many objectives for conducting a review, including:

- to gather data to inform stakeholders of the degree of success of the project, activity or inactivity
- to gather stories for publication in magazines or the press
- to find people to blame (which may be an unstated objective of many public enquiries)
- to assess the input of individuals, to allocate rewards or praise.

There are no doubt other objectives as well, but if we are interested in learning lessons, we can add a learning objective to the review, namely:

- to identify lessons that have the potential to improve performance in future.

We have looked at definitions of lessons and lessons learned in Chapter 2. We have defined lessons identified as 'a recommendation, based on analysed experience (positive or negative), from which others can learn in order to improve their performance on a specific task or objective'.

The lessons identified process is therefore a process of analysing experience (positive and negative) on a task or objective, in order to identify lessons from which others can learn. The process needs to have the following characteristics:

- *be grounded in solid performance data*: Lesson identification has to be based on facts and analysis of facts. If you are trying to learn from a project budget overrun, then you need to know where the budget was overspent, and by how much. If you are reviewing the effectiveness of a policy, you need a good assessment of its effectiveness. If you are drawing out lessons from a safety incident, you need to investigate the facts before you can draw any conclusions (as described in detail in Chapter 13).
- *look at positive as well as negative experiences*: Any review of project activity or tasks should acknowledge what has gone well, as well as the components that were a struggle or a challenge.
- *refer back to the objectives of the task, project, activity or initiative*: Lessons often arise from positive or negative differences between what was expected and what actually happened, and are derived from a review of what was supposed to happen, what actually happened, and the

reason for the difference. That means you need to compare the actual result with the objective. However, even if there were no difference, you can still identify learning: 'Our objective was to deliver this project in 24 months, it took 24 months, but could we do it even better in future?'

- *separate experience from opinion, as much as possible*: A lesson is different from an opinion or an idea, because it arises from actual experience and is (as far as possible) an objective reflection on the results. You make it objective through good facilitation, through the use of skilled objective investigators and interviewers, and through accepting inputs from as many as possible of the people who were involved in delivery. That means that lessons from group or team activity should be identified by the complete group or team.
- *generate unique and distinct lessons from which others can learn and take action*: Each learning point should be an individual lesson, and careful attention should be given to making it usable and actionable. This last point is so important that we will give it an entire section on its own.

Aiming for the 'quality lesson'

A lesson identified was defined in Chapter 2 as being:

> A recommendation, based on analysed experience (positive or negative), from which others can learn in order to improve their performance on a specific task or objective.

A key phrase in this definition is 'from which others can learn'. A lesson is something you can teach to others. So a good lesson is something which is easy to teach, and easy to learn from. One of my clients coined the phrase 'specific actionable recommendation' to describe a good lesson.

A lesson needs to be specific enough that others can learn from it. It is surprising how often people fail to do this. I read a lesson last week that said: 'To do X properly will require time, resources and effort'. Is that a lesson, or is it a platitude? Is there anyone anywhere who thought X could be done in no time, with no resources and no effort? The group or team or person who wrote the lesson knew what message they wanted to convey, but still ended up with something so non-specific as to be useless.

A lesson needs to be actionable – people need to be able to take action based on what you have written. You need to avoid such generalities as

Principles of lesson identification

'Y needs to be better in future'. As well as being more specific about 'better' (what sort of better? better in what way? what elements need to be better?), you need to think about how this 'better Y' will be achieved. What needs to be done? What actions need to be taken? ('An updated process description is needed for Y, including the following...').

Finally it needs to be a recommendation, rather than an observation. I went through some documents recently which were purported to be lesson identification documents from an absolutely crucial project, and half of the 'lessons' were observations. They were statements such as 'the team encountered great difficulty in Z'. This is not an identified lesson; it is a description of what happened. If we are to learn from what happened, in order to help future teams approach Z more effectively, we need to know why this team encountered difficulty, what the root causes of that difficulty were, and what their recommendation would be for other teams to avoid that difficulty. There has been no analysis in this 'description of what happened', so there can be no specific actionable recommendation.

Examples of poor lessons

Let us look at some examples of poor lessons, so we can learn what a good lesson looks like.

The statements below (all taken from real organisations) have been chosen from various lessons learned documents. As you read them you will note that they are frequently historical statements, not recommendations. None of them meets our definition of a lesson identified:

> Organisations may not have anticipated or prepared for the effects of this risk.
>
> The integrated information campaign was delayed by the lack of advance planning.
>
> The boat was late arriving, and the engineer was not suitably qualified.

Additional work is needed to make each of these statements into a lesson that can be actioned. In each case, we need to ask: 'What have we learned? How do we ensure organisations are prepared? How do we ensure future campaigns are not delayed? How do we ensure future boats arrive on time and with suitable personnel on board?' So we need to do a bit of analysis, and look for root causes, and then phrase the lesson for future use. We need to turn it into a recommendation.

The three lessons below, also taken from lessons learned documents, are non-specific and full of unquantified terms like 'early' and 'more', so they do not meet our standard for a lesson identified:

> A project of this kind will require extensive planning, which must be started early.
>
> Budgets for this sort of work need to be larger.
>
> Make sure the project team is adequately staffed, with all the key skills represented, from the pre-tender stage.

In each of these cases we need to ask for more specific information: How much planning? An extra year? An extra day? How early should it start? How much bigger should the budgets be? Double? Treble? 100 times bigger? What is adequate staffing? What are the key skills? And so on.

Remember, all of the above have been taken from real lessons learned systems of well-known organisations. Without guidance, people often write lessons like the above.

So how about a good lessons learned example?

You can find many of these in lessons learned databases, where there has been an attention to lesson quality. For public domain examples of good lessons, I recommend the NASA lessons database (*http://eo1.gsfc.nasa.gov/miscPages/fppd-ll.html*), from which I have taken this example as an example of a well-written lesson:

> A 10% budgetary reserve is inadequate for a technology validation mission. The EO-1 experience suggests that 15% is a minimum and 20% would be preferred. Three characteristics peculiar to technology validation missions require this additional reserve. Accurately assessing the maturity of an advanced technology is very important. Considerable reserve can be quickly expended in maturing a technology to reach flight status consistent with the aggressive schedule typical of such missions. In a related way, using reserve to overcome whatever difficulties may be encountered in the fabrication of 'first-time' flight hardware is another activity that can quickly consume considerable reserve. Lastly, the exact performance needed to effectively validate the advanced technology may not be fully understood until rather late in the definition process and this may increase the cost of the spacecraft.

Recommendation:

Future technology validation missions should carry a minimum budgetary reserve of 15% at the Confirmation Review.

Why do I like this example? Because it is clear, quantified, written as a recommendation, backed up with a good argument and context and, most importantly, someone reading the lesson would know exactly what to do in future. It also leads towards action, namely changing the review guidelines for technology valuation projects.

Stories and lessons

Even the clearest lesson benefits from being illustrated with a story. The learning is being identified within a context, and it helps to understand the context when reviewing the lesson, so that you can know whether it applies within your context. Therefore a story can support a lesson by providing valuable background and context. That does not mean that the story is necessarily a lesson in itself. We can tell stories for many reasons, such as interest, entertainment and scandal, without necessarily deriving lessons from them. There is a lot of interest in story telling within knowledge management, but my suggestion is that story telling alone – with no analysis of the learning points, identification of the lesson, and movement into action – is not an efficient way of learning. Everybody listening to the story would need to draw their own conclusion, and the most qualified person to draw the conclusion is the one who lived through the story. Why not let that person share their conclusion as something that others can learn from? Stories are easiest to learn from when they carry a learning point that is a specific, actionable recommendation.

Self-identification of lessons versus lesson identification processes

Sometimes you may need to set up a system whereby people identify lessons themselves, and add them into a lessons database. I am not a huge fan of self-identification – I think you capture only a small proportion of the lessons this way, and the lessons you capture are often superficial. This is partly because we often 'don't know what we know': the issue of the unknown knowns.

These are the things that people know without realising – the unconscious competencies. It is very often the deep-lying technical learning that is of real value to others. But how can someone share knowledge if they don't know they know it? Few people are self-analytical enough continuously to analyse their own performance to look for the learning points.

The people who have the knowledge are often unaware that they have it. The people who need the knowledge are often unaware that they need it. Without an effective learning identification process, the crucial knowledge may never be transferred. We need a process of helping people know what they know.

The best process to help people identify their lessons is *questioning*. The most effective means of identifying and transferring lessons is through dialogue – via Q&A. Through a Q&A process, knowledge suppliers become conscious of what they have learned, and once they are conscious of this, they can explain it for the benefit of others. This works for teams as well. Teams have an unconscious competence in the way they work effectively together, and the knowledge of success and failure is often held in common. It is like a jigsaw, and each team member holds one piece. However, these learnings don't come to light until you start to ask questions. Once you start a process of dialogue and start discussing the reasons behind why things happened, the team will often piece together their learning as a group activity.

So is it possible to self-identify lessons? Well, it is possible, but suboptimal. If you have to use self-identification, for example if there is a very strong cultural reluctance to analyse and question performance publicly, then:

- Give people a template to fill in (we will look at the nature of this template in the section on lessons learned databases, Chapter 10).
- Give them some really good lessons examples as exemplars.
- Be prepared to follow up with them if the result you get is poor, which it probably will be. My experience of self-submission is that no matter how carefully you set out the template, people fill in very few of the boxes, and will fill them in with history, non-specifics and non-actionable comments. Peter Kemper makes additional points in Chapter 15 about the unreliability of form filling to capture lessons.

My recommendation would be, as far as possible to use a dialogue-based process to identify lessons, such as an interview, a debrief, an after action review, a retrospect, a learning history or evaluation. These question-based processes are described in Chapter 5. In the section below we talk about the questioning approach that lies at the heart of these processes.

The questioning process – the metaphor of the tree

If you are facilitating a questions-based or dialogue-based process for identifying lessons, you will find it very useful to have some sort of questioning structure, to help you operate the process. It is very easy to get pulled off course by the flow of conversation, and without a good structure, you can lose control of the process. The tree analogy described here is a good way to build a structure, and can be used to keep track of individual interviews, team retrospects and after action reviews.

The tree structure recognises three sets of questions, with three purposes, represented by the trunk of the tree, the branches of the tree, and the 'fruit' at the end of the branches. The trunk, branches and fruit represent, respectively, the topic of the conversation (the event being reviewed), the various subtopics that need to be explored, and the lessons you finally identify. The purpose of the questioning is to work with the individual or team to identify the branches, to explore each one, and to 'pick the fruit'.

The *trunk* of the tree represents the basic purpose of the interview: the task, process, policy or project in question. To identify the branches that come off from the trunk, which you want to explore, you can ask 'What' questions. These are questions in the past tense such as:

- What were some of the key issues?
- What were the success factors?
- What worked well?
- What did not work well?
- Where were the challenges and pitfalls?
- What would you approach differently if you ever did this again?

Once you have identified these branches, use open questions about the past beginning 'How' and 'Why' to gain an idea of where the learning points might be. A useful acronym to remember for helping you to ask open questions is WET – Why? (or What?) Explain? Tell? You are trying to get to root causes, and the '5 whys' (Wikipedia, n.d.) may be useful (see Chapter 13). Or ask questions such as:

- Why do you think you were so successful?
- What did you put in place to ensure success?
- What was missing, that caused that to happen?
- What makes you say that?

- Can you explain how you achieved that?
- Can you tell me about that?

As you approach the root cause, you will identify when you are getting close to a learning point, and when you can move to the third type of question.

The 'fruit-picking' question comes once you have identified a point where the individual or team has learned a lesson, and you have got to the root cause behind the lesson – the factor that made it go well, or the element that made it fail or go badly. That is when you ask a future-tense question – a 'What' question – to require the person or team to analyse the learning and create a recommendation. The question might be one of the following:

- What would be your advice for someone doing this in future?
- If you were doing this again, what would you do next time?
- If you could go back in time and give yourself a message, what would you tell yourself?

This future tense 'what' question is vital, and needs to be asked. By getting people to provide advice and recommendations, you are moving beyond exploring the history of the project, and starting to think about what should be repeated, or what should be avoided. You are starting to identify the process improvements. This is also the point at which you ensure that any recommendations the team or interviewee give are specific and actionable. Don't be satisfied with woolly answers; press for specifics. Don't be satisfied with unquantified words like 'lots' or 'enough'; press for measures.

Once you have 'picked the fruit', you then move on to the next 'branch' and explore that, until either the tree (the topic) is completely explored or you have run out of time.

Case Study 4.1 Interview about communications during a merger

This is a simple example from a real interview. The theme is communications during a merger. The interviewer asks a 'trunk question' to identify some of the highlights; the things that have gone well. He then questions each of these highlights asking branch questions, and finally a 'fruit-picking' question:

Principles of lesson identification

'Trunk' question	What stick out in your mind as some of the key highlights?
Answer	One of the things that was very popular with the employees was a Q&A system we had on the intranet.
'Branch' question	Why was the Q&A so successful? How did you make it work?
Answer	The Q&As were posted on the intranet for all employees to see, within one day of announcement. There was a slot for employee questions...
'Fruit' question	So if you were advising someone about setting up a Q&A system, what would you say?
Answer	I would say that you need to set it up from day 1 – from the first announcement – and...

This questioning structure and the principles covered in this chapter form the basis for all the lesson identification processes that we will discuss in the next chapter, whether they are designed to identify lessons from an individual, a small team conducting a task, or a large team conducting a project or programme.

Roles and accountabilities in lesson identification

There are a series of roles and accountabilities for lesson identification, and they really need to be clearly understood within the organisation, so that everybody knows the part they have to play. Some of the roles and accountabilities in a project-based organisation are listed below.

- *Project managers or team leaders* are ultimately accountable for making sure that the lessons from the project or team are identified. They need to make sure that the team know what lesson identification process will be applied, and to check that they actually are applied. They need to make sure that there is adequate resourcing for lesson identification, and to make sure that it is prioritised, and not overtaken by more urgent, though arguably less important, operational activity. Project managers or team leaders may also want to take the lead in approving any lessons that are escalated to the rest of the organisation, as discussed in Chapter 7. In a large project or team, they often delegate responsibility for monitoring lessons learned activities to a 'project knowledge manager'.

- *Project knowledge managers* usually play an active role in making sure the lesson identification processes happen. They set up review meetings, make sure facilitation is provided, and that people attend. They monitor lesson learning activity, lesson identification and the closure of any associated actions. They do not have to identify all the lessons themselves but they have to make sure that the lessons are identified. This role within the project team is not necessarily fulltime nor named, but much as project managers need somebody to run the risk management system or to operate the project planning system, so they need somebody to look after the lessons learned system. Knowledge managers need to be relatively senior and have credibility. They need to be:
  – good listeners, facilitators and communicators
  – familiar with the concepts of knowledge management
  – good at influencing
  – good at thinking strategically
  – experienced within the company and business
  – well networked.
- Any facilitator or investigator who is appointed to help with a lesson identification process will make sure that the process runs smoothly, and that all processes operate well. In some cases, a project might appoint a learning historian who works full time at facilitating lesson identification. At the end of the project this person will produce a learning history, and a complete set of identified lessons. Obviously this is a significant investment in personnel, but where the project is the first of many, and the learning will have major applicability, it may be worth investing this resource. For example, a construction organisation that is looking to expand into the Far East might employ a learning historian on the first pilot project, so that the maximum knowledge can be gained from this for the benefit of all subsequent projects. The learning historian will identify lessons by interviewing people, facilitating after action reviews and retrospects, and generally

by documenting what happens and what has been learned. In BP, on the offshore oil rigs, this task is taken by a learning or technical limit coach who works within the project team to make sure that the technical limit and learning methodology is carried forward into day-to-day learning during operations. In the US Army, a small team of personnel ('operations officers') may be assigned to any one major operation to carry out learning. This team is called a 'combined arms assessment team' and plays this facilitation or learning role.

- Learning facilitators and learning historians should be experienced and credible people, not necessarily high in the hierarchy, but with several years of practical, hands-on experience. When young graduates were put in this role on the oil rigs, it was found that they lacked the credibility and depth of understanding to play the role, so experienced blue-collar workers were used in the role instead.
- If the investigation is of an accident or incident, then this may be carried out by a specialist investigator, as described in Chapter 13.
- A project planning to deliver a specific outcome for a stakeholder population (such as a project team within a government department implementing a new policy) may also commission an evaluation study to evaluate the impact made by the project. Here they will employ or commission a research team to conduct the evaluation. This team will be tasked with either identifying lessons or evaluating impact to allow the project team to derive its own lessons.
- Team members have accountability within the lesson identification system as well. They are accountable for taking part in the lesson identification process, and for volunteering any additional lessons that they may recognise. They have a responsibility to be open and honest.
- There may well be a central learning coordination or knowledge management team, to help support lesson learning throughout the organisation. This team is accountable to ensure that the projects, operations and teams have the skills that they need to identify lessons, and have access to technologies and resources for those lessons to be stored, shared and reused.

Reference

Wikipedia (n.d.) 5 Whys, *http://en.wikipedia.org/wiki/5_Whys*.

5

Processes of lessons identified

The previous chapter discussed some of the principles of lesson identification, and in this chapter we describe how these principles can be put into processes that are used by the team or organisation.

There are a range of processes for lesson identification. Participants in the lessons learned survey introduced in Chapter 1 reported the use of the following processes:

- project-related reviews: post-project reviews or retrospects (28 responses)
- after action reviews (17 responses)
- individual (ad hoc) submission (7 responses)
- external reviews (6 responses)
- learning from incidents and events (5 responses).

Project-related reviews and after action reviews are the most common, and these are described in detail below. We then go on to discuss individual learning interviews and learning histories, including external reviews, learning from incidents and events, and data gathering. Please feel free to skip the detailed description of processes that you have no intention of following! Because this book is designed as a handbook, I have gone into detail of issues such as process facilitation to give you the capability to do these things for yourself. This will be very valuable for process facilitators, but others readers will be forgiven if they move on.

Post-project reviews or retrospects

The retrospect is a robust, tried and tested approach for capturing lessons at the end of a project, project stage or sub-project. It was initially developed within BP in the early 1990s, but has spread to very many organisations, in many sectors and markets. Although it has some features in common with the after action review, it takes longer, goes into greater depth, makes sure that each individual on the team has a chance to contribute, and expresses the learning in terms of recommendations and advice for future projects.

Most organisations have some form of review after their major project activity. A post-project review, appraisal or audit will generally look back at what happened in the project and what was achieved compared with the objectives. Was the project completed within budget or over budget? Was it delivered to time? Was it delivered to specification?, and so on. A good appraisal or audit might go further than this, and look at the root causes behind things that went wrong, and may even look at the root causes behind things that went right. Sometimes the project leader alone writes this review, although often it will involve the project team as well.

Where the retrospect differs from typical post-project appraisal is that it goes beyond a historical review, and looks to the future, asking, 'How do we avoid the problems in future projects?', 'How do we repeat the successes in future projects?' and 'What can we give the next project team to help then deliver a perfect project?'

Setting up retrospects

It is important to schedule the retrospect at the end of the project or project phase, before the team disbands or moves on to fresh work, and before history becomes post-rationalised. Hold the retrospect while memories are fresh and the project team is still available. It can be useful to combine the end-of-project retrospect with an end-of-project celebration, and treat it as a close-out exercise for the team. Everybody on the team should attend, and the client or customer for the project can be invited if appropriate. You may feel uncomfortable discussing project performance with the client present but experience has shown that the value added can be enormous.

Somebody who was not part of the project team should facilitate the retrospect. The better the facilitator, the better the outcome of the retrospect will be. Under no circumstances should the project team self-facilitate; somebody external should steer the process, ask the awkward questions, and make sure any undiscussables are discussed. Find a good facilitator who has a clear idea of the retrospect process and the purpose of the exercise. Retrospects are not complicated meetings, but they do need attention to purpose, attention to behaviours and, in particular, attention to the quality of the lessons which are identified. Understanding and following the process is key to a successful outcome.

It is very powerful if you can find somebody who will reuse the lessons – perhaps the project leader for the next similar project – and get them to attend the retrospect as an observer. The presence of this person will give the process a greater level of focus and legitimacy, and they can help make sure that the lessons which come out of the retrospects are expressed as useful recommendations and advice. For example, one organisation we worked with had just won a bid for major construction work in a former Soviet country. The project manager invited the bid manager from a neighbouring country to attend their post-bid retrospect. As he was in the process of compiling a bid himself, many of the lessons could be transferred immediately, and he was able to probe for useful, specific, actionable detail. Knowledge reusers should not facilitate the retrospect; they will have their own agenda which should not be allowed to dominate the meeting, as they will not be the only users of this knowledge. The facilitator needs to make sure that all the knowledge from the project is captured, not just the knowledge that will be immediately reused in the next project.

The retrospect process

Introduction

The first step in a retrospect is to set the scene by discussing the purpose, process and ground rules for the meeting. Make it clear that the meeting is held to capture the lessons, in order to help future project teams. The purpose of the meeting is not to assign blame or praise, but to make life easier for the next project team. Also make it clear what you will do with the output from the meeting, especially if you are recording it. Once retrospects have become an established standard process, you don't really need to set the scene, but where this is a new process then you may need to be careful as you set up the beginning of the meeting.

Project objectives

Next you need to review the objectives of the project itself. Ask the project leader to start off this section. If they can find the original terms of reference, this is good because it adds some ground truth and reminds everybody of what they set out to do in the beginning. It is worth reviewing whether these objectives changed, whether there were any hidden objectives, and whether people had any personal objectives. Depending on the scale of the project, this may take between five and 30 minutes.

Project achievements

The next stage involves looking at what actually happened in the project, and what was achieved at the end. Again, try and get to ground truth: what was the actual expenditure compared with the budget? What was the actual timing of the project compared with the plan? What feedback have members of the team had from the clients or customers on the quality of the work? In a long or complicated project you may need to draw a flowchart of what happened before you can start to analyse it.

Identify issues

The next stage is to identify the success factors and challenges that need to be analysed, and from which lessons need to be drawn. There are a number of ways to do this:

- You can ask people to identify successes and challenges before the event, so you have a short list before the retrospect itself. This is effective if you can get the team's attention, but often people do not give it much thought. It is the only way to identify success factors and challenges from people who cannot attend the event.
- You can ask the attendees to brainstorm their top three (for example) success factors and top three challenges and put them on individual Post-it Notes, which can then be grouped into themes for analysis.
- You can map out the flow of the project, including the major tasks, activities and steps, and then ask people to identify the activities that were particularly successful or challenging. Prioritise these areas for further discussion and analysis.
- Ask people in turn to identify their successes, and then prioritise them. This is difficult to facilitate as people often start discussing the items rather than just identifying them.
- Ask people in turn to identify their successes, and discuss them in the group as each one is identified. This method ensures that everybody contributes, but it may be difficult to manage the time.

Discuss issues and identify learning points

If we use the tree analogy for structured questioning from Chapter 4, the identification of issues described above involves mapping out the branches of the questioning tree. This next section – discussing issues and identifying learning points – is analagous to exploring the branches and 'picking the fruit'.

Take the issues one by one, in order of priority, and hold a group dialogue on each one to find the root causes of the success – ('Everybody, why do you think this was successful? What did you do to ensure success?') – and continue the dialogue to ask how the success can be repeated in future ('So what would you recommend to a team doing this in future, to repeat the success? If you were doing it again tomorrow, what would you put in place?'). I like to discuss the success factors in order of priority first, and then to discuss the challenges in order of priority.

This section of the retrospect can take between 10 and 20 minutes for each person present (so if six people are present, it could take between one and two hours). The purpose of the discussion is to come out with good quality lessons, namely specific, useful actionable recommendations for future projects, which will allow them to reproduce the identified success. Good firm facilitation may be needed here, otherwise the meeting can easily degenerate into a discussion on what people liked about the project (or, worse, into a blamestorming session), or can generate woolly and vague lessons. With firm facilitation, some very useful material can be developed for future teams.

Case Study 5.1 is an extract from a real retrospect, and shows this questioning process. The third question from the facilitator is the forward-looking, 'fruit-picking' question that identified the lesson.

Case Study 5.1 Example extract from a retrospect

Facilitator   Mr X, what was the top success factor for you?

Mr X   One of the successes for me was the flexibility we had, so that when we hit problems in the project, we always had a back-up task we could go to.

Facilitator   How do you achieve that degree of flexibility? [Much discussion ensued]

The Lessons Learned Handbook

Group	Detailed planning meant that everyone understood what was the next job to move on to if the current one was held up.
Facilitator	What should future projects do to achieve that degree of flexibility?
Group	Authority to change jobs should be pushed out to the individual team leaders. Also the team needs to hold a three-day look-ahead every day, so they know what jobs to move on to.

During this process you may also identify procedures, documents or other artefacts which may be useful for future projects. For example, if a success factor was the clear definition of roles at the start of the project, then you can ask for a copy of the role definition document, which can then be reused by managers of future projects as a template or starter for their own role definition document.

Occasionally, when reviewing a difficult project, conflict may arise. Different people at the retrospect may have different perceptions of what happened to cause a breakdown or failure in the project. Arguments can start, tempers can rise. The way to turn conflict into a positive outcome is to ask the question 'What should we do *next time*, in future projects, to ensure this breakdown or failure does not happen again?' In many ways it does not matter precisely what happened this time, or whose fault it was, so long as everybody is agreed on how to do it better next time. In fact, the question 'what should we do next time?' is the most powerful question to ask in retrospects. It is almost worth writing this question on a flipchart, and sticking it on the wall. The whole purpose of the retrospect is finding lessons that can be reapplied next time, or in the next project.

A further step can be to ask the project team what they can give to the next project to help them perform. Obviously they can give them the results of the retrospect, but they may be able to offer them documentation, advice, templates, plans, lists of contacts and so on.

Closure

As a closure exercise, at the end of the retrospect, I like to go round the room and ask people to rate their satisfaction with the project, as 'marks out of 10'. Sometimes, if the project has delivered a great result through struggle and hardship, I asked them to rate their satisfaction first with the product, and second with the process they went through. This satisfaction rating exercise has three main purposes:

- It allows people to express their feelings about the project without having to use emotional words, and given that the people have been reliving the projects during the course of the retrospect, discussing the highs and lows, it is quite good to 'even out' with an overview statement of how they feel.
- It allows you to identify the outliers. If everybody was giving the project 8 out of 10, apart from one person who gave it 2 out of 10, then you need to understand why.
- It allows you to ask a supplementary question: What was missing from the project which would have allowed you to give it 10 out of 10?

Retrospects for large or complex projects

It is difficult to hold a retrospect for more than about 15 or 20 people. Retrospects are based on a process of facilitated group dialogue, and it is hard to have dialogue if the group is too large. However, it is unusual that you would have so many people collaborating on shared objectives. Larger and more complex projects tend to be broken up into sub-projects, with smaller teams delivering sub-objectives. In this case, you can hold separate retrospects for the sub-teams, and then one for the leadership team of the project, to review how well the sub-projects were coordinated.

Recording retrospects

Knowledge has credibility when it is expressed by credible people – people with experience. Knowledge captured in the form of quotes or soundbites from the project team can be seen as being the voice of experience, and can be used in the form of stories to add context to the identified lessons. If you are going to add context and credibility in this way, then the retrospect needs to be recorded carefully – recording people's own words as closely as possible, the stories that give context to the lessons, and who said what. You either have to take very detailed notes (speed-writing) or, if possible, you should audio-record the event. Although some people may worry about having a tape recorder present, you can reassure them that it is only for transcription purposes, that any recordings will be destroyed after transcription, and that nothing will be published without giving the retrospect attendees the opportunity to edit it first. However, the amount of learning that comes out during a retrospect is so huge, that often audio-recording is the only practical way to capture it all.

It can also be useful to summarise some of the key retrospect lessons and stories on video. At the end of the retrospect, when the lessons have been identified and discussed, ask a few of the more eloquent speakers to summarise what has been learned, and what they would recommend for future projects based on that learning. These small video summaries can be a good and engaging way of recording some of the key lessons.

After action reviews

The after action review is a well-established, well-regarded and well-documented process to identify lessons from an activity. The after action review process was initially developed within the US military, but has since been applied in a wide range of industrial settings.

After action reviews are short, structured, review meetings, conducted to draw out lessons from a task or activity. The term is also used in some organisations for longer review meetings held at the end of projects or programmes. In this book, I refer to these bigger-scale processes as retrospects. After action reviews are useful for helping individuals and teams gain immediate performance feedback, and to identify and carry forward lessons for immediate application. Additional benefit may be in the identification of lessons to be shared with other teams – though most benefits are for the team. After action reviews do not go into very great analytical depth, and so are useful for reviewing short-turnaround activity or single actions. They are short and focused enough to carry out daily, perhaps at the end of a meeting or shift. For example, a refining company might use after action reviews after each shift during maintenance activity.

Scheduling

After action reviews are best carried out for events – entire small actions or distinct parts of large actions – with measurable objectives, which have clear beginning and end points, and where there's been a significant variance (positive or negative) from expectations in terms of measured results, such as time, cost, quality and completeness. They will deliver most value on an activity that will be repeated in the very near future by the same team. An after action review should be run as a proper meeting, and schedule space needs to be allocated for it ahead of time.

Attendees

Attendees for an after action review should be the team members who were involved in the activity. Other people can be included if they have something to add, for example if they were observing or coaching the team, or if they will be involved in this activity in the future. When in doubt about whether someone should attend or not, be exclusive to the team. The basic rule is that the review is carried out by the team, for the team.

There's no need to engage an external facilitator to hold the after action review. Decide which team member will facilitate and take notes.

Structure

The structure of an after action review is very simple. It consists of asking five questions, which are answered through dialogue within the team:

- *Q1 What was supposed to happen?* The first question is asked about the objective of the activity, and the target performance. We have often found that the first few times you ask this question, people turn out to have been confused about the objective or the target, or else no clear objective was set. One of the by-products of after action reviews is that they promote objective-setting.
- *Q2 What actually happened?* The second question looks at actual performance. If you are conducting an after action review, you need to establish 'ground truth' with this question. You are looking to determine reality rather than opinion. If we take the 'tree' analogy for questioning, the answers to this question map out the branches of the tree. This is the point at which you have to ensure that you avoid opinion and emotion. It is very easy for the discussion to become heated. Try to avoid that by always coming back to 'ground truth': what actually happened and what is the evidence to support it.
- *Q3 Why was there a difference?* The third question seeks to understand why a particular result was achieved. Perhaps you did better than expected; perhaps you did worse than expected; perhaps you met your target. What were the factors that determined the result? Another way to ask this question, if the first way doesn't work, is, 'What went well, and what did not go so well?' The US Army after action reviews sometimes asks for 'three up, three down' – three items that worked better than expected, and three items that worked worse than expected. In the tree analogy of questioning, this question (or, more commonly, set of questions) explores the branches.

- *Q4 What have we learned?* The fourth question asks about the learning, and should be expressed in terms of what will be done differently the next day (or, in cases of over-performance, what should be repeated the next day). Here you move from analysis of the activity to 'what we are going to do about it'. In the tree analogy, this is the 'fruit picking' question.
- *Q5 What action needs to be taken?* Once you have decided 'what we are going to do about it', you need to assign the action to ensure it gets done. Much of the time the action lies with the team. If the team cannot fix the action, there needs to be an escalation route. In many textbooks the after action review process is described with four questions. We prefer five, to highlight the move from lesson identification to lesson learned.

The answers to these questions can usefully be recorded on a one-page pro forma, or a marked-up flipchart, which can be collected for future reference. Note that although we show the five questions in sequence here, what typically happens is that the reply to Question 2 will identify a few areas to be discussed, and then questions 3, 4 and 5 are asked for each of these areas in turn (as shown in Figure 5.1).

Figure 5.1 After action review structure

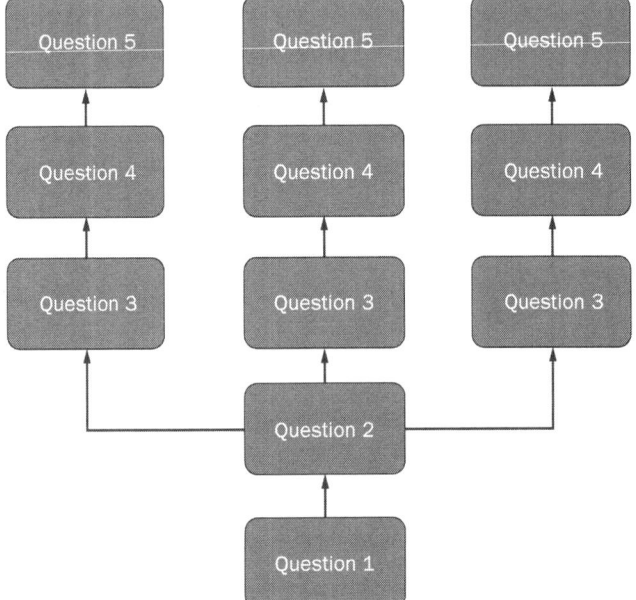

Processes of lessons identified

Case Study 5.2 shows an example of an after action review from a refinery maintenance exercise, with the level of task detail to which after action reviews may be applied. This example comes from a shift team in Singapore, who were installing trays within a refinery unit (a tray is a particular piece of equipment inside a refinery column, and needs to be fitted by someone working at height).

Case Study 5.2 After action review Q&A for a shift team in Singapore who were installing trays within a refinery unit

Q1 What was supposed to happen?	1. To install trays, with weir heights and downcomers within tolerance.
	2. To hold tray assembly in place with appropriate hardware, e.g. bolts and nuts, clamps, washers, slide fasteners, etc.
Q2 What actually happened?	1. Tray clearances were not within tolerance.
	2. There was a shortage of hardware.
Q3 Why was there a difference?	1. Workers were using measuring tapes to adjust the clearances resulting in a need for repeated re-working.
	2. Workers were transporting the hardware up the column in bulk, resulting in hardware being misplaced, dropped, or not following vendor's instruction on the appropriate type of hardware to be used.

57

Q4 What have we learned?	1. Use standard blocks prepared to the required dimensions for adjusting weir height and downcomer clearance.
	2. Put all the appropriate hardware in place on the tray sections at ground level before transporting up the column.
Q5 What actions need to be taken?	1. Request the workshop to construct a series of standard blocks.
	2. Update daily orders for tray installation.

Although the learning here is only about small things – tray tolerances, clamps and washers – an increased ability to avoid small mistakes, based on day-by-day routine learning, can give a massive performance improvement at the end of a project.

The after action review process works well in an open, blame-free, inclusive environment. You need to set ground rules for after action reviews, for example:

- Aim for openness, not hiding any mistakes.
- There should be no hierarchy – everyone's input is equally valid.
- Leave preconceptions and prejudgements at the door.
- The focus of the exercise is learning, not blame or evaluation.
- Respect and listen to each other.
- Everyone who was involved in the activity should take part in the after action review.
- No outsiders should be present; nobody should be there to audit performance or learn how to conduct an after action review.
- Deal with the significant issues and the significant objectives, not trivia.
- Disagreement can be constructive and needs to be explored.
- Don't rush to solutions.

Individual learning interviews

An interview is the most effective way to identify lessons from a single person. The UK military, for example, holds debrief learning interviews with all senior commanders returning from the battle zone, to derive the top level lessons from a command perspective. A review of an incident, or an evaluation of a major piece of work, may also involve knowledge capture from a number of people through a series of interviews, the results of which are then compiled using the process described below as the 'learning history'.

Interviewing is a form of dialogue, a Q&A process, which continues until the interviewer feels they have reached a valid piece of knowledge, expressed as a specific actionable recommendation, based on ground-truth. Interviewing is a skill, which can be learned and developed through practice. Interviewing in the context of safety incident investigation is covered in Chapter 13.

Preparation

Careful preparation will help you and the interviewee, and will give a better end product. Allow at least an hour for a normal interview, or several hours for an in-depth interview with a senior person (such as the military interviews with returning commanders). Make sure the interviewee knows why you are interviewing them, who you are, what the process of the interview will be, how long it will take, and what you will do with the output. Make sure you know who they are, why they are important, and what their role was in the activity being reviewed. Do a bit of background reading so you understand some of the context, and know some of the technical terms.

For crucial interviews, or if the interviewee is very senior, the ideal is to work in pairs if you have the resources. There is a lot to think about in an interview: the recording, the note-taking, the quality of the answers, the next question to ask, and so on. One person can be in charge of the questioning process, and the other in charge of note-taking and recording equipment but also keep an ear open for the quality of the answers (whether they are specific, measurable, usable and so on).

Explain the process

Be clear about the topic, purpose and ground rules of the interview. You are interviewing this person to identify their lessons, rather than to critique their performance or obtain a magazine article. You therefore need to make it clear to them at the start, precisely what you are interviewing about. For example you might say, 'I would like to interview you for about an hour on what you have learned during the Tiger project, in the area of managing such a complex transnational activity.' You then need to explain what will happen to the output, who will write it up as lessons, what their role is in validating the lessons, and how the lessons will be carried through into action. For example, 'The purpose of this exercise is to help future transnational projects deliver the same degree of success as yours, by building on what you have learned. I will write up the lessons, ask you to review them in about a week's time, and when you have approved them they will be passed (via the lessons database) to the project review board, which will make any necessary changes to our project process.'

You will also need to explain some of the processes that you will use, ask permission to record, and reassure the interviewee that they will have the right to edit the output before it is published. We generally assure interviewees that any recording (with the exception of video clips) will be for transcription purposes only, and ask them to be as open as they like during the interview in the knowledge that they can go back and reword things later. Make sure they realise that their lessons will be attributed to them, and the interviewee will be given full credit for their knowledge.

The interview process

The interview process then consists of following the questioning structure explained in Chapter 4 using the metaphor of the fruit tree. During this process you will be helping the interviewee uncover the key bits of knowledge that they may not even realise they know (the unknown knowns). As the interviewer you have dual responsibility – first to the interviewee (to help them become aware of what they have learned), and second to the ultimate audience (by making sure that the lessons you help the interviewee identify will be specific, relevant and actionable). You must ask questions on behalf of the audience and manage the conversation so useful answers emerge. You are looking for the secrets of this person's success, and what they have learned from their experiences. You don't know what these secrets are, and the interviewee may not fully know either! So there is no point going into the interview with a list of questions and expecting simple answers – the questioning is a process of exploration.

Keep track of the structure

You need to keep good notes, in order to follow the questioning structure. When I am conducting an interview, every time the interviewee mentions a new theme, success factor or challenge – which will become a new 'branch' in the interview 'tree' – I put a big asterisk against it in my notes. Then I can keep checking back and make sure all of these branches have been explored: 'Mr X, earlier you said that teamwork had gone well – can we just explore that for a bit? *Why* do you think the teamwork was so good?', and so on.

Use your listening skills. Your role is to ask short questions to allow the interviewee to express what he knows. Make sure your listening:speaking ratio is 80:20 or greater. Listening is not passive, however. You need to use 'listening skills', for example:

- suspending judgment (not trying to analyse if what is being said is right or wrong or whether you agree with it)
- not interrupting (especially when you are recording the interview)
- paraphrasing (repeating back what someone has said to you using your own words and context, to check for understanding)
- purpose stating (saying why you are asking the question)
- encouraging (making eye contact, smiling and nodding).

Sum up

Once you have explored all the branches and 'picked all the fruit' (identified all the lessons), a good way to sum up the interview is to ask the interviewee to summarise the top three or five lessons of the project. We find this question very useful in prompting a good summary:

> As a summary of what we have been discussing (and this will probably be repeating some of the things we have been through), if you were speaking to somebody who was just about to start on a similar project tomorrow, what would your key points of advice be?

It is good to capture this section of the interview on video or audio file. You may want to give the interviewee a couple of minutes of preparation or thinking time, before running the cameras.

Identify the documents

As you go through the interview, make a note of any key documents that the interviewee mentions (for example, 'Bill produced guidelines for the inspection visits, which we found very useful'). Ask whether you may have an electronic copy of these to include in the final product ('Can you get me a copy of Bill's guidelines?'). Again, you can put a mark against your notes whenever a key document is mentioned, and this allows you to refer back to them at the end ('You mentioned the following key documents; X, Y and Z – do you think you would be able to email these to me by the end of the week?'). These documents may be very useful to attach to the lesson.

Make a recording

A vast amount of knowledge will come out from an interview. They are a rich source of guidance, anecdote, experience, advice and story, and you need to capture this material in an equally rich way. You really need a complete verbatim transcript from which to work, so it is helpful to record the interview with a digital voice recorder. A simple pocket dictation machine will be sufficient, and can sit fairly unobtrusively in front of the interviewee. Make sure whatever recording machine you use is compatible with the transcription service you will employ, that the batteries are fresh and you have spares. Ideally have a spare recorder. I was interviewing earlier this year, and managed to tip a cup of tea over my digital recorder. However, I was prepared, and had a second recorder in my bag.

Take detailed notes as well. Speed-written notes are useful in two ways: as a non-technical backup to the recording equipment and as a way for you to follow the interview 'tree' as it branches. Detailed notes are also valuable as a backup if your recording equipment fails, or if the recording is of poor quality. Speed writing is a useful skill for the learning engineer, but it is a tiring process. Make sure you have a large notebook and several sharp HB or B pencils. Buy a new notebook for each series of interviews.

It may be useful to take a photograph of the interviewee. Some organisations put the originator's photograph in the lesson document.

Telephone interviews

Sometimes it will be impossible to conduct the interview face-to-face, for example if you are interviewing the members of a global team. You will then need to interview them by telephone. The process will be the same, but a telephone interview requires far more concentration than face-to-face interviews. You may also need to spend additional time setting up the context and establishing rapport. It is not so easy to 'break the ice' in a telephone interview, and you will need to go through who you are carefully, and explain who commissioned the lesson identification and what you will do with the output. As you conduct the remote interview, be careful to explain what you are doing in more detail than you would if you were meeting in person. For example, 'I would like to ask one or two context-setting questions, and then we will go into more detail' or 'Can I please follow up on that point, because I think this would be a very useful area to discuss further'.

Take care with recording. Often the best you can do is to place a tape recorder next to a speaker phone or video-conference loudspeaker. Better, is to buy a splitter which takes an audio stream from a telephone handset socket. You should use a speakerphone or a telephone headset, so you have both your hands free for taking notes. Do not audio tape a telephone conversation without the person at the other end being aware beforehand that you are going to tape the conversation.

Learning histories

Sometimes a project is so large or dispersed, or contains people who are so busy and unavailable, that it is impossible to schedule an end-of-project retrospect with everyone in the one room at the same time. An alternative approach, the 'learning history', collects lessons through a series of one-on-one interviews with project team members. For example, a manufacturer and retailer of branded products went through a major mergers and acquisitions programme, which was conducted by a fairly small team of very high ranking staff. It proved impossible to bring the team together for a retrospect, so a learning history was conducted. Each of the high-ranking team members was interviewed individually, and the lessons were collated into a single document.

The scale of the learning history depends entirely on the number of people you need to interview, and the larger the project team you interview, the more working days you need to allow for the process. A good rule of thumb is to allow about one working day for each person interviewed, so a learning history based on interviews with ten people will take about ten working days to collect, edit and complete.

Given the resource required to undertake learning histories, they are only applied to the most important and strategic projects.

The learning history process

The process of the learning history is based on interviewing, and the analysis, collation and distillation of the results are a very large part of the process. If the scale of the learning history is large, you may need a team of interviewers and analysts. A learning history from a project with a project team of ten people can be done on your own; from a project with more than 20 in the extended team you might need some assistance.

The process is as follows:

- *Set the expectation.* This is going to be a big effort. Make sure you have prominent sponsorship from the project customer and project leader.
- *Identify the people to interview.* These need to be key players who had 'skin in the game'. The project leader, the main client, the core project team and key sub-project team members should all be interviewed.
- *Put together a group of people to conduct the learning history.* They will need journalist skills, interviewing skills, analysis skills and writing skills.
- *Conduct the interviews.* Use the interviewing approach presented above, and the 'tree' structure for questioning described in Chapter 4.
- *Transcribe the interviews.* Select the quotes you will use from the interviews, and check them with the interviewees.
- *Analyse the results.* Identify the common themes, and distil the common lessons. This can be a huge job. In a big exercise, you can spend several days on this step.
- *Feed back the results* if you can, then get the interviewees together in groups, starting with the sponsor group, and discuss the results of the history with them, reflect on it together, and talk through its implications and the lessons you have derived. The lessons can be updated with any new insights that arise during the conversations.

As an example, a learning history on road safety was conducted in BP Turkey in 2002. Through a long programme of cultural change, BP Turkey had been able to reduce its road traffic fatality and injury rate by a staggering amount. In order to help other parts of the group to replicate this success, BP Turkey commissioned a learning history to capture lessons about improving road safety. Twenty-seven people were interviewed in Turkey, and the interviews were transcribed and compiled into a collection of lessons for others to learn from.

Evaluations and assessments

Evaluations and assessments may often include a component of lesson learning, but are primarily an assessment of the results of the programme against its objectives. This is the definition of evaluation used by the UK Department for International Development, which was originally used by the OECD Development Assistance Committee:

> The systematic and objective assessment of an on-going or completed project, programme or policy, its design, implementation and results in relation to specified evaluation criteria.

This definition doesn't mention learning, although of course lessons can be learned from the results of the evaluation. Evaluations will generally contain a large element of data gathering, using quantitative and qualitative methods to assess the success of the programme. Data may well be gathered from a large number of stakeholders and the implementation team. The UK government conducts impact evaluations on many major policies to assess the impact the policy has had. As an example, a policy such as introducing smoke-free legislation (banning smoking in public spaces in England) would be followed by a detailed impact assessment to see whether this legislation is being complied with, whether it is improving the health of workers in public spaces, and whether it has had an impact on the prevalence of smoking in general.

The World Bank suggests a number of questions that an evaluation will address:

- Does the programme achieve the intended goal?
- Should this pilot programme be scaled up? Should this large scale programme be continued?
- Can the changes in outcomes be explained by the programme, or are they the result of some other factors occurring simultaneously?
- Do programme impacts vary across different groups of intended beneficiaries (males, females, indigenous people), regions and over time?

- Are there any unintended effects of the programme, either positive or negative?
- How effective is the programme in comparison with alternative interventions?
- Is the programme worth the resources it costs?

However, the key question that we address in this book, and the key question for improving the work of the programme team, is not included in this list: 'What are the lessons that will allow us to build better programmes in future?'

The best way to answer this question would be to hold a retrospect for the programme team, and to use the results of the evaluation as input to the retrospect. Evaluations as described above are often processes for measuring results, rather than processes for identifying lessons.

Incident investigation

Incident investigation is a special form of learning exercise, focused on something that has gone badly wrong. This may be an accident, an environmental breach, a major upset in production, or some other big problem. Details of incident investigation as applied to safety are presented in Chapter 13.

6

Writing down the lessons

Once a lesson has been identified, it generally needs to be written down. Though there are processes for transferring lessons directly from one person to another (as we will see in Chapter 11), and sometimes action can be taken without writing anything, much of the time the lesson will be written down somewhere and stored. This allows it to be transmitted to others who need to learn from a lesson, or to others who need to take action based on the lesson. Writing the lesson down allows it to be stored in a database where others can find it, or entered into a shared wiki, from where it could be tracked from identification to action.

Recording the lesson is a step where value is often lost. A lesson that is not documented well, through ambiguity, lack of clarity, lack of context or lack of detail might not be reapplied and is therefore a wasted opportunity for performance improvement. A cursory glance through most shared learning systems shows that the quality of lessons varies considerably, from extremely useful to completely unhelpful. Lessons learned systems, like other systems, will experience the problem 'garbage in, garbage out', and we need to eliminate the 'garbage in'.

In this chapter we will cover some of the principles and best practices in lessons documentation.

Each lesson stands alone

One of the first principles for effective lesson learning is that you need to capture lessons individually. There is no point in bundling together all the lessons from a single project, as the people searching for lessons will be searching for lessons to help with a specific issue, risk or task. They would like to find all the lessons associated with that issue, risk or task in the same place. They don't want to go back through 20 or 30 project reports, looking through the lessons learned section of each one. In order to make it easy for the lessons to be found, you need to split them into individual lessons, and store them under themes or topics in the lessons learned database or wiki.

However, if each lesson is to stand alone, then each one needs to be captured with sufficient context that it can be read and understood in isolation. You cannot assume that the reader of the lesson will also have read the complete project close-out report; the lesson must contain as much context and detail as it needs to be understood in isolation.

The lesson needs to be easy to follow and well structured

The stand alone principle is a reflection of a more basic underlying principle: you are writing lessons for an audience. You need to have that audience in mind as you write down the lesson. You need to make sure it is very easy to follow and laid out in a logical way. In drafting a lesson you need to keep asking yourself, 'Will a person who I will possibly never meet or speak to be able to pick this lesson up, understand it and then apply it in their situation without referring back to me?'

One of the better ways of doing this is to reflect, in the structure of the documented lesson, the process you went through in identifying the lesson. If the lesson was identified through any of the processes listed in Chapter 5, the chances are you went through a process of:

- identifying the theme (what went well, what could have gone better)
- revisiting the situation in which the lesson was learnt
- analysing the difference between what was expected and what actually happened
- looking for the root causes of the lesson
- deriving a recommendation for the future.

If this is the process by which the lesson was identified, then it could easily be used as the structure for documenting the lessons. The description of the lesson would therefore contain sections that:

- *classify the lesson according to the theme to which it refers*. It is likely that in this section you will make use of an existing taxonomy to classify the lesson. What is the lesson about? Is it about bidding? Contracting? Personal protective equipment? Of course it may be about more than one topic, and you may want to enter a series of keywords, which will allow people to find your lesson when searching for it in future.

- *describe the context in which the learning happened*, for example the project and its objectives, or the constraints or the particular circumstances under which the lesson was learnt. We will discuss in the section below how much context you need to give – this can vary given the nature of the lesson. The guideline is only to write sufficient context to support the insight or recommendation that you are making.
- *describe the event itself, from which the learning occurred*, for example an accident, something that went wrong, or a particularly successful task or piece of process.
- *describe the root cause analysis that you went through*, or list the root causes that drove the success or failure. This is important – the people who validate the lesson need to know the rigour of your root cause analysis, and may even need to dig down another level or two for deeper causes if necessary.
- *describe the lesson itself*, expressed (as we suggested in Chapter 4) as a 'specific actionable recommendation', fulfilling all the criteria for a quality lesson that we set out in that chapter. This is the clear identified lesson expressed in terms of what should be done in the future, and it is supported by the other sections, which give the reader a degree of context so they can understand how the lesson might be applied in their own situation.
- *describe any actions arising from the lesson*; we cover actions in Chapter 7.

Very often the best way to write a lesson like this is to start with the specific actionable recommendations, and then work backwards to describe the context within which the lesson can be set. If the lesson was identified at a retrospect, then the facilitator's notes from the retrospect will be very useful indeed for documenting the lessons. If you have audio-recorded the retrospect or after action review, then the transcript from the recording provides good raw material for documenting the lessons, although the transcript will almost certainly need to be rewritten to make it more understandable.

If you set up a lessons learned database, then set up the forms in the database to cover the sections above (and also the metadata described below). This will help people ensure that the right level of context and detail is provided when the lessons are documented in the database. However, we cannot assume that people will necessarily fill in the forms correctly, as pointed out in Chapter 15.

How much context?

How much context and background description do you need to give to a lesson? I know I said above that you should provide just enough to support the insight or the recommendation that you are making, but how much is 'just enough'? The person reading the lesson needs to make sure they understand the context to know if the lesson applies to them, so the amount of context you need to provide is determined by two things:

- the simplicity or complexity of a lesson
- the similarity of the context within which it will be reused.

Let us start with the first issue: the simplicity or complexity of the lesson. Some lessons will be much easier to document than others. A simple lesson, such as the need to fix a particular piece of equipment or subtly to modify a process, can be documented in a few lines, perhaps with an attached diagram or photograph. A more complex lesson, such as how to negotiate a contract with a foreign government or how to raise a child, will be much harder to write down, and will need more than a few lines and a diagram. In BP, the first type of lesson is referred to as 'low-context' and the second type as 'high-context'.

Low-context lessons:

- are relatively simple and straightforward
- can be explained thoroughly but concisely in writing
- can often be expressed in the process flow, or a diagram
- may be captured using a template.

High-context lessons:

- are complex and difficult to explain
- are more easily explained than written down
- can be situation specific
- may be captured using stories.

Both types of lessons have value, need to be identified, and need to be documented in any lessons learned system. However, the degree of background explanation and context you need will be much higher for the high-context lessons. In reality, of course, there is a continuum between the two, and any lesson will need a certain degree of context.

Who is the audience?

The second factor that determines how much explanation and detail you need to add to your lesson is the similarity of the context in which it will be reapplied. A lesson generated by a team and applied within the team will be reapplied within the same context. Everybody will understand what it means, understand its importance, and understand the jargon and acronyms. The lesson can be documented in a few lines. However, if the lesson is likely to be reapplied by a different team, in a different project, perhaps in a different country, maybe several years in the future, then you cannot assume that everybody will know what you are talking about. You will need a lot more explanation of terminology, and of the context in which the lesson was identified.

At the extreme end of the spectrum, for a high-context lesson that will be reused by another team you may need to illustrate your lesson with some detailed stories. This is where we start to bridge the gap between lessons learned and storytelling, as described in Chapter 4.

Attachments

Many lessons benefit from attaching diagrams, flowcharts, pictures, stories, video clips or other attachments. If you feel a document will help the reader understand the lesson, then attach it. However, you have to make sure that you are legally able to share this accompanying documentation. There may be confidentiality agreements, secrecy agreements or 'Chinese walls' within an organisation that need to be considered and honoured.

Quality assurance and validation

Because of the need to remove the 'garbage in, garbage out' problem that besets so many lessons learned systems, and because important lessons may have significant impact across the organisation, there may need to be a quality control and validation step before the lesson is finally published. The project knowledge manager, for example, may want to check the wording of the lessons to ensure that they are clear, that the recommendations are specific and actionable, and that there is a sufficient amount of context. He or she may also want to weed out duplicate lessons, or lessons that merely reinforce what is already known. The project manager may want to check the wording of the lessons, to ensure they accurately reflect the nature of the project. In some cases there may need to be a legal review of lessons, especially if they have any bearing on product safety and may be discoverable in any future legal process, or if they are contract-related lessons from a project where penalty clauses are being invoked. In cases like this, it may be very important to consider carefully the exact wording of the lesson.

Different teams and different lessons learned systems have different validation processes. Some teams hold a lessons learned meeting involving senior people in the project regularly, for example once a month. During this meeting they will review all lessons, validate the good ones, send the poor ones back for further work, and agree and assign the actions. In other teams, there is a workflow by which lessons are validated first by the knowledge manager, and then by the project manager or a delegate.

The exact nature of the validation and quality assurance process is not as important as actually having a validation and quality assurance process in the first place.

Lessons must lead to action

As discussed in Chapter 2, lessons must lead to action. Documenting a lesson is not enough – there must be actions which arise from the lesson, which must result in change. In the next chapter we will discuss actions.

7

Taking action

We have argued above that lessons have to lead to action if they are to be implemented, and that lessons that remain in a database – or, even worse, remain in a report on the library – are often ignored. With no action, nothing changes.

This was brought to my attention by one of our more blunt-speaking clients, who returned to us one day and said 'your retrospect process is rubbish'. When we asked him to explain further what was behind his remark, he explained that the same negative lesson had turned up in all three of the past three retrospects of a particular type of project. Obviously nothing had changed, and no progress had been made. We explained that this was not a problem with the retrospect process itself: the process was correctly identifying the lessons from the project, but no actions were being taken as a result of the lessons identified. The clients had introduced retrospects, but had not considered the rest of the learning loop – how to carry the lessons forward into changes in the way the organisation operated.

If we can assign an action to a lesson and then track that action there is a much greater chance of that lesson making a difference, and making a change. However, there are a number of questions to be answered before we can introduce a system for assigning actions to lessons. We need to know whether actions are always necessary, what sort of actions are necessary, who will assign them, who will carry them out, and what will happen if the actions need to be referred to a higher level.

Will there always be an action?

This is a common question – will there always be an action associated with the lesson? I think in the vast majority of cases there can be, but maybe this is not immediately obvious. I was asked this question recently when working with a client in the aerospace industry. The client was introducing a lessons learned system, and I was stressing how important it is to assign actions to the lessons. He said, 'I think you will need to show me. I will open our lessons learned database, choose a lesson, and see whether an action would be possible.'

We went to the lessons learned system, and opened one of the most recent lessons. It was about welding on the company's aircraft structures, and one of these teams had recently introduced a new method for welding, which was faster, more efficient, and produced equally strong results. This is definitely the sort of lesson that needs to be replicated; if other teams can reproduce this approach to welding, then costs will fall and construction times will decrease, with no compromise to technical integrity. But how can we carry forward this lesson into action?

In response to my questions, my client told me that the organisation used welding guidelines, had an induction process for new welding contractors coming into the organisation, and that welding was supervised. So actions could be taken: the welding guidelines needed to be updated, the new method needed to be introduced into the induction process for new welders, and the supervisors needed to be briefed with the new methodology and asked to pass it on to the welding staff.

It is not always as simple as this. Imagine that a contractor was working on a building site, and had a near miss where he nearly fell from the scaffolding. He hadn't been following key company guidelines for working at height, he had failed to attach his harness, and he tripped and nearly fell to his death. An incident analysis is held, and lessons derived. But what is the lesson? Is it 'You have to follow the procedures for working at height'? If so, there is no action. There is already a clear set of procedures for working at height, and these don't need to be changed, updated or restated in any way. Instead you need to get to the next level of root cause, and find out why the contractor had not followed procedures. Had he not been properly trained? Did he not understand the gravity of the subject? Had he never seen the procedures? Why had his fellow workers not noticed what he was doing? If we dig a little bit deeper we may well find that action *is* needed. Perhaps there needs to be a refresher for staff on safety behaviour, or a better safety induction process for new contractors; perhaps the issue of 'passive bystanders' needs to be brought up for the next health and safety briefing.

There are certain cases where no action is necessary:

- *When the learning merely reinforces a previous lesson, or existing guidelines.* If guidelines have been written for a process or procedure, the guidelines were followed and the procedure was successful, some teams may record this as a lesson. However it is not a new lesson, and no new action is needed. The lesson has reinforced the existing guidelines, but not created new ones. The only possible action in this case might be to record the incident as a case history in support of existing lessons, but if the procedures are well established, they may need no more support.

- *When the occurrence was a 'one-off' and is very unlikely to happen again.* Perhaps there was a successful intervention when conducting a particular task or doing a particular activity which will never be repeated on the project, and which is unique to that project. It may be worth discussing the lesson among the team to acknowledge that this was a successful intervention, but there won't be any actions arising, as this circumstance will never recur.
- *When the lesson is a 'non lesson'* – when it is an observation, or a comment, and there is no lesson arising. For example a team might discuss at a retrospect that 'the schedule changed at the last minute, and we had to work very hard over the weekend in order to accommodate this'. The weekend working may have been a burden, but in fact the staffing of the project took account of the possible last minute schedule changes, and the weekend working had always been retained as an option to deal with this. So in fact things went according to plan, even though it was a burden at the time. There is no specific lesson arising, and no action.

However, usually we can find some sort of action to help embed and institutionalise the learning from the lesson. Some of the types of actions are discussed in the next section.

What sort of actions are needed?

There are probably six main types of lessons that arise from actions:

- fixing a problem
- investigating further
- documenting a procedure or process
- updating a documented procedure or process
- updating a training course, other training or e-learning material
- circulating the lesson for others to decide on an action.

Fixing a problem

These are the simplest and most obvious actions. During a review of performance, such as an after action review, a team might realise that things could have gone better if a particular problem had been fixed, and it is within their power to fix it. The lesson is obvious: fix the problem. As an example, a team might look at their performance in constructing a particular type of machinery, and realise that they could have constructed it much faster if they had had two hydraulic wrenches, allowing two teams to work in parallel. They have two more pieces of equipment to construct. The action is also obvious: buy or lease a second hydraulic wrench. These sorts of 'problem fixing' actions could involve:

- buying new machinery or equipment
- mending machinery or equipment
- replacing machinery or equipment
- training staff
- hiring new staff
- changing a contract
- changing an organisational structure.

Investigating further

Sometimes it is impossible in the lesson identification meeting to get to root cause, through lack of data or lack of access to the right people. In this case, further investigation may be needed, and the action associated with the lesson will be an action to investigate further. For example, a drilling rig was encountering repeated problems with a particular piece of machinery designed to clear small fragments of rock from the drilling mud, which were not being cleared in a particular section of the well. This was reviewed at the end of well retrospect, no root cause could be identified, and the action was to send samples of the rock fragments away for further laboratory investigation. After lab inspection, a detailed chemical analysis of the samples came up with a solution, and the lesson could be updated with a new, more informed, action. 'Further investigation' actions may include:

- observing the situation more closely next time
- setting up an investigation study
- setting up a laboratory study

- collecting more data
- involving an expert
- holding a peer assist (see Chapter 11).

Documenting a procedure or process

When a team or project has done something for the first time, they have learned a considerable number of lessons. The best thing to do with these lessons is to document them in a procedure. For example, staff in one organisation were trying the process of 'partnering along the supply chain' for the first time. During a series of retrospects and interviews, very many lessons were identified, but practically all of the actions associated with these lessons were the same one, namely to build a 'guide to supply chain partnering', where these lessons could be combined into a valuable reference set. The action to document a procedure could result in creating one or more of the following documents:

- operational procedures
- 'doctrine'
- guidelines
- checklists
- best practice
- technical standards
- training materials
- case studies
- 'tips and hints'
- FAQs.

Updating a procedure or process

When you are working with a well-documented process you will find that most activities are already covered by procedural documentation. In this case, any new lesson may well represent an improvement to or identification of a pitfall in existing procedures. The action associated with the lesson is therefore to update the procedures. For example, in Case Study 2.1 the action was to update the drilling guidelines. Other actions the staff might take, for other lessons, could be to update rig procedures, standard operational procedures, recommended procedures, drilling manuals and the company drilling wiki. In most cases, before updating a procedure, there may be some management-of-change process that needs to be gone through. You cannot just change procedures willy nilly – there needs to be due process to make sure that the updated procedure doesn't cause more problems than it solves.

Updating a training course or other learning material

This action often accompanies the previous action of updating the procedure, to make sure that training and e-learning material is fully up to date with current knowledge.

Circulating the lesson for action by others

In some cases, the action cannot be taken locally, but may need to be taken at very many different sites around the organisation. An example is a safety lesson, where a particular hazard has been identified at one site. Although the hazard can be removed at that site, the lesson also needs to be circulated to all sites with similar operations, so they can check whether a similar hazard exists. Or maybe a defective piece of equipment has been identified, and all sites which use that equipment need to be notified so they can go and check it, see if it is defective, and replace it if required. One of the risks to an effective lessons learned programme is that this action of 'circulate for local action' becomes the default, and that the other sites come to treat it as 'circulate for information' rather than 'circulate for action'.

Case Study 12.1 describes how Ford addressed this risk in its best practice replication programme by requiring staff at the sites to report back what they had done as a result of the lesson that had been circulated. They could make one of five statements:

1. The lesson is not applicable at this site for the following reasons ... and therefore no action has been taken.
2. The lesson is not economically feasible at this site for the following reasons ... and therefore no action has been taken.
3. The lesson has been previously incorporated at the site.
4. The lesson has been adopted at the site, with the following benefits.
5. The lesson is currently under investigation.

By requiring this report, Ford made sure that actions were taken at a local level as a response to the lesson. A similar requirement to report back what is being done as a result of the circulated lesson could be very usefully introduced to health and safety incident reporting and lessons management systems (see Chapter 13).

How do you decide the action?

It is not always easy to decide what action needs to be taken. Very often the success or failure is influenced by many factors, whether superficial or deep. There may be symptoms and root causes. Taking actions to address the symptoms may be helpful in a superficial way, but will be nowhere near as helpful as addressing the root causes. So whatever lesson identification process you apply, you may need to dig deep below the symptoms and identify the key learnings and actions that need to be taken. A skilled facilitator or investigator should be able to do this, and this establishment of root cause is particularly important in accident or safety investigation (see Chapter 13). In more day-to-day lesson identification, such as after action review, the root causes may sometimes be missed.

As an example, let us consider a bid team reviewing an unsuccessful bid. Its members need to understand why the bid was unsuccessful, and whether there are any changes that need to be made to ensure that future bids are successful. Perhaps they decide that they have overpriced the bid, and lost out on price. Taking this learning superficially, they may decide that for future bids of this type, they need to decrease the price in order to be successful, and the action needs to update the bidding guidelines to reflect this. But why was the price set at this level in this case? What process did team members go through when setting the price? Why did managers not pick up on this pricing issue when they carried out the pre-bid review? At the time, it seemed that the pricing was realistic, but with hindsight it looks as if conditions have changed in this marketplace, and that this bid could usefully have been offered at a lower price as a market-entry 'loss leader'. Perhaps the root cause was that there was no discussion early in the preparation of the bid to decide on a pricing strategy, and that the sales force already operating in this market had had no input to the pricing. In which case, the action is that the bid preparation process needs to be altered to include one more step: the preparation of a pricing strategy, fully informed by the knowledge of the relevant sales force.

Or let us consider an investigation of a near miss, when an operator started up machinery when the hand guard was open, by pressing a switch which he was not supposed to press. What is the action? Is it to retrain him and other operators on that machine? Is it to notify all sites where that machine is present, and ask them to train the operators? Is it to disable the switch? Is it to redesign the machine, so there is an interlock between the switch and the hand guard? Quite possibly it is all of these actions, and potentially more as well. When a lesson is identified, the facilitator or investigator needs to do enough root cause analysis to know the underlying factors that caused the success or failure, and needs either to lead a discussion to assign effective actions to each cause, or to pass the lesson on to a person or group of people who will assign the action. Chapter 13 gives an example of actions assigned to a safety lesson, where an air hose was attached to a nitrogen line.

Who assigns the action?

The actions associated with lessons are usually (but not always) suggested by the team or individual who identifies the lesson, with the help of the facilitator or investigator, if there is one. Many lessons learned databases contain a field for assigning an action, and whoever fills in the lesson on the database will fill in this field. However, there's often a validation step for lessons by somebody senior, and that senior person will look at the action and see whether it is realistic, really addresses the root causes, and has been assigned to the correct person.

There are alternative approaches to assigning the actions. In one organisation, teams hold a lessons learned meeting regularly, often once a month, involving senior people in the project. During this meeting they review all lessons, validate the good ones, send the poor ones back for further work, and agree and assign the actions for each validated lesson. In another organisation the output from retrospects is reviewed within a week of the retrospect at a meeting of the senior engineers, who prioritise the lessons and assign actions for the most important ones. In many non-military government departments where lessons are derived from independent reviews and evaluations, senior civil servants have a meeting, go through the evaluation reports and decide which actions need to be taken as a result.

However the actions are assigned, there needs to be a recognised process and workflow to ensure that an action is assigned to each lesson, and that somebody is made accountable for delivering against that action, by a specific date. The decision about who should take the action and what the action should be needs to be taken by someone in the organisation who has the authority for assigning actions. You cannot have junior engineers in a manufacturing plant assigning actions for the head of procurement, for example. However, sometimes those junior engineers identify an action that would have considerable benefit to the organisation as a whole. In this case, there needs to be a process for escalating the action to a level where it can be assigned by someone with the appropriate level of authority.

Escalating the action

If all of the actions associated with the lessons can be applied within the project, there's no need for escalating the action. The actions can be assigned by the project manager, who already has the correct authority to require people to do things. Whoever manages the lessons learned process for the project can then make sure that the lessons are closed out. However, sometimes the action is for somebody outside the project to take. Maybe the project has identified a company process that needs to be updated or written. Maybe an equipment redesign is needed. These are actions for either the company process owner or the person who holds the contract with the equipment supplier. Neither of these people is in the project, and the project manager doesn't have authority to tell them what to do. The action has to be escalated to a level where the required authority lies. For example, it might lie with the head of projects, the leader of a particular functional discipline, or a member of the senior level steering group. In each case, this person or group of people has to be bought into the lesson learning process, realise that lessons need to lead to changes, and be willing to assign actions to the correct people so that these changes are made.

This escalation route is shown in Figure 7.1.

Actions to update a company process are taken by the respective process owner. For example, an action to update company welding guidelines needs to be assigned to and taken by whoever owns those guidelines – the chief welding engineer or similar.

Actions to create a process have to be assigned to a process owner, and there is usually somebody well placed to own the process. For example, a new process for improving the process of bidding might be owned by the head of the bid team. He or she might delegate the actual documentation of this process, but they would own the process, and sign off the document.

Actions to buy new equipment would be held by the procurement department, and actions to modify existing equipment would either be held by procurement or by whoever holds the contract for that specific equipment.

Figure 7.1 Local and company learning loops

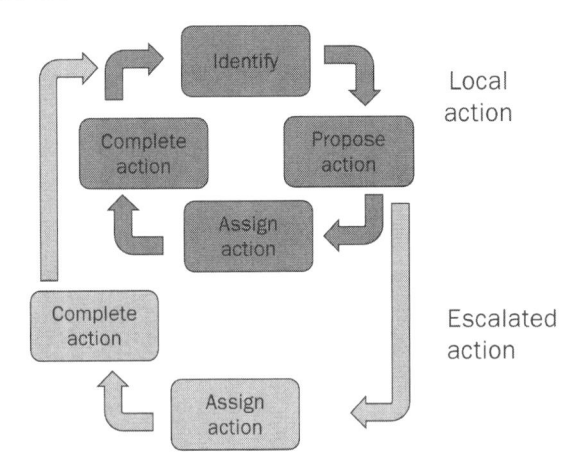

Actions to notify the organisation of a new learning would be assigned to the head of the relevant function or community of practice. For example, notification of new safety lessons would be circulated by the head of safety. Notification of new engineering lessons would be circulated by the head of the engineering community. Notification of new sales lessons would be carried out through the sales and marketing community of practice.

Closing lessons

Once the actions associated with a lesson have been taken, we can consider the lesson 'closed'. The lesson can then be archived from any lessons learned database, as it has now been incorporated into process. Anyone looking for the most current knowledge will find it in the updated processes, or else in the 'open' lessons, where the actions have not yet been taken.

It therefore makes sense to keep only the open lessons in the lessons database, and to archive the closed ones. The percentage of closed vs open lessons, and the time it takes to close lessons, are both important metrics for monitoring how well the learning loop is operating (see Chapter 12).

So lessons lead to actions, and actions often include the update of process. In our next chapter, we will investigate the issue of process ownership and process update.

8

Process ownership and process update

Learning implies memory. If there is no memory, learning cannot take place. Babies learn through stimuli and responses from the outside world, by comparing them to existing mental models held in their memory and updating their mental models over time. But where is the memory of an organisation? You cannot rely solely on the memory of employees to be the totality of the memory of the organisation, as employees come and go, and the human memory is, after all, a fragile and fickle thing. In addition to this human organisational memory, we can make a strong case for organisational structures, operating procedures and processes also forming a core component of organisational memory. Processes and procedures are built up over time, and represent the company view of 'how we do things'. Employees follow the processes, and repeat 'how things are done'. The processes hold and propagate the patterns for behaviour and the way work is conducted. If the organisation is to learn, these processes must evolve over time.

The concept of evolving processes as part of the learning loop is recognised by many learning organisations. One of the learning professionals in the UK military asked me, 'What is doctrine, if not the record of lessons learned?' (Doctrine is the military term for process, or for operating procedures.) The head of common process at BP explained the BP common process as being 'the embedded knowledge of how to operate'.

In the previous chapter we looked at the actions that might need to be taken as a result of identifying a lesson:

1. Fix a problem.
2. Investigate further.
3. Document a procedure or process.
4. Update a documented procedure or process.

5. Update a training course, other training or e-learning material.
6. Circulate the lesson for others to decide on an action.

These actions form the link between the identified lesson and the resulting changes in the organisational memory – the organisation structures, processes and procedures, and training programmes. In this chapter, we will investigate further actions 3, 4 and 5, and move into the topic of process ownership and process update.

It has been a theme of this book so far that learning has to lead to action, and that action has to lead to change. If nothing changes, nothing has been learned. Changes can be as simple as fixing a piece of machinery, acquiring a new loan, hiring a new person, or buying a new tool. In these cases, there is a change to the inventory of the company, a change in the concrete assets. However, very often what needs to change are process and procedure. In this case, there is a change in the intellectual assets of the organisation. But who makes the change, who authorises it and how is it recorded?

For lessons to lead to change in process, the following things need to be in place:

- a set of documented processes and procedures
- owners of these processes and procedures
- engagement by the owners in the learning process.

Let us start with the issue of process ownership.

Who owns the processes?

Perhaps we ought to start with deciding what process ownership actually means. Process ownership is a key component of many management approaches such as business process improvement, six sigma and lean manufacturing, and there are many definitions available in the literature. The definition below is a simple one:

> A process owner can be defined as the person accountable for maintaining the definition, and the quality of a particular process. They don't have to operate the process themselves, but they need to make sure that the people who do operate the process have access to the documentation they need to operate the process in the (currently identified) best possible way.

Let us continue the example from the last chapter of the lesson about the new approach to welding. The process owner for welding in the organisation would be the person accountable for maintaining documentation on welding process and best practice, and therefore the person you would go to in order to update the welding guidelines.

Similarly a marketing company might have a process owner for television marketing, another for print marketing, and another for online marketing. The reference (in the definition above) to the need to operate the process in the 'best possible way' implies that the process owner knows enough about the business context to know what 'best' means for the business, and that they understand what the key performance indicators and metrics are for the process. If it also implies that if improvements to the process are identified, the process owner is accountable for reviewing them and updating the process as a result. So the process owner is a key actor in the learning cycle.

Exactly who owns the process depends really on the maturity of the process, and the structure of the organisation. Some examples of process owners are listed below.

Technical authorities

The technical authority role is used in many engineering organisations, for example NASA, to ensure that all operational decisions are made with reference to technical engineering knowledge and expertise. Technical authorities might be individuals such as the chief engineer, the chief electrical engineer or the head of marketing. They are generally the owners or custodians of internal standards and policies, and so can be considered to be a process owner where a process is fully defined by an internal standard. When a process has been standardised, it is likely to be very well understood and unlikely to change much. Changes to standards are rare, and caused only by major deviations from normal operations. It therefore makes sense only to give process ownership to the technical authorities in the case of mature and well-established processes.

Subject matter experts

The subject matter expert doesn't necessarily have any line authority in an organisation, but has intellectual authority based on their expertise.

This expert is the company-designated person in the organisation who has the greatest expertise in a specific technical topic (although the term is sometimes used to describe somebody who has expertise in the particular subject matter, rather than the person with the greatest expertise). It therefore makes sense to make them the process owner, because, in theory at least, they know more than anybody else about the topic related to the process. It makes sense for the subject matter expert to be the process owner for any process that is mature and well defined enough for a single person to grasp it in its entirety.

Community of practice leaders

Communities of practice will be covered in more detail in Chapter 11. The leader of the community of practice is the person who coordinates community activity and makes sure that community knowledge is compiled and documented. It makes sense for the community of practice leader to be the process owner, when the process knowledge is dispersed within the community rather than held by any one person. This will be the case when a process is relatively new, is being widely applied in the organisation, and where knowledge about the process is still evolving. So rather than a subject matter expert being able to hold all the knowledge in their own head, the community of practice owns the process, and the ownership role is coordinated by the community of practice leader. There may often be cases where the community of practice can themselves keep the process documentation up to date, perhaps by using a wiki or another collaborative tool. The community of practice leader, in this case, acts as the coordinator and editor.

The research and development team

Sometimes the process is very new, has only recently been identified, and is in the process of being developed through a programme of trials. Here the R&D staff own the process, and use the R&D programme to explore and define the process.

Figure 8.1 shows that as a process matures, the ownership of the process will change.

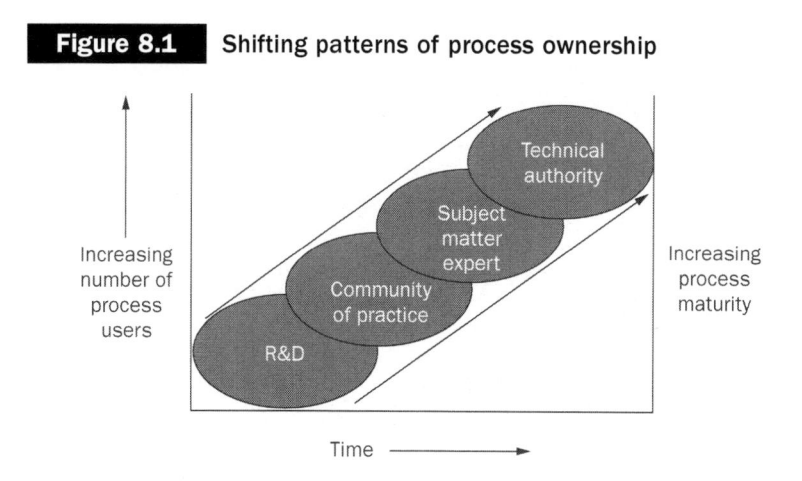

Figure 8.1 Shifting patterns of process ownership

Local vs company process owners

Processes can be owned at more than one level. There may be a company approach to a particular process, for example, and a local variant which is tailored to the local context, market or legislation. For example, there may be a company marketing subject matter expert who is the process owner for marketing within a particular organisation, while the Latin America office contains the local marketing subject matter expert who is the company expert on marketing within Latin America. Figure 7.1 illustrated that there may be learning loops at more than one level in the organisation, for example a local learning loop and a company learning loop. Similarly there can be process ownership at local and company level, built into these two learning cycles. A lesson from Latin America may need the local process owner to update their Latin American marketing process, or it may be a sufficiently important and generic lesson that the company process owner has to update the whole company's marketing process. We will come to this point below when we talk about validation and escalation.

The role of the process owner

These are some of the responsibilities of process owners:

- monitoring the development of knowledge within their specific area of expertise

- ensuring that new identified lessons are collated and shared from significant pieces of work
- promoting peer assists and personal connections between projects to share tacit knowledge of the process
- developing and publicising process guidance documents relating to their specific process
- developing, and agreeing with management, corporate standards for their specific process
- updating guidance documents, best practices and standards for the process as required
- ensuring that guidance documentation is made available to all users
- publicising and rolling out new lessons and updated process documentation
- monitoring use of any relevant process documentation, and acting on feedback to improve it
- liaising with the leader or coordinator of any community of practice that covers the process
- monitoring the organisational performance in the application of the process.

Engagement with the learning cycle

For the lessons learned approach to work properly, the process owners need to be thoroughly engaged with the lessons learned cycle. They need to be incorporated into the lessons process, and to be intellectually and emotionally engaged with learning. They need to know they are part of the learning loop, see themselves as an integral part of the cycle, and have a vested interest in making sure that the learning loop operates successfully.

You might think that a process owner is going to be naturally engaged with the learning. If they are accountable for making sure that key processes are documented in the best possible way, and using the best possible knowledge, then they should welcome any suggestions for improving the process. However, this doesn't always happen. Dealing with a constant stream of process improvement suggestions could be seen to be a nuisance and distraction, and a process owner who has just released a beautifully documented process may not be keen to revise it immediately, if at all. We were working recently with an organisation that had spent a lot of time developing best practice on managing subcontracts. The company had set up a task force, conducted a programme of knowledge collection, created very impressive guidance documents, and tied these into a training course. When we asked them how they intended to refresh this document and keep it updated, the reply was 'We are not sure we have even thought about this'.

It is vital that process owners are fully engaged with the learning cycle if lessons are to be learned properly. The management of the company needs to make sure that the roles of the process owners, whether they are technical authorities, subject matter experts, community of practice leaders or R&D managers, include the expectation that processes will not only be documented, but also be continuously updated as new lessons become available.

The corollary to this is that there needs to be a close link between lesson identification and process update. They need to be part of the same workflow.

Lessons workflow

In Figures 2.1 and 7.1 we have already seen diagrams that attempt to describe the flow of lessons, from activity through identification, to action and process update, and so back into activity. We can add the accountability dimension to this and start to think in terms of a workflow for lesson learning.

Figure 8.2 is an example of a workflow illustrating how a lesson could flow around a hypothetical organisation. The workflow will differ depending on the organisational context, where the lessons come from (project review, incident reporting, evaluation and so on) and who needs to be involved, and the vertical dimension of this figure represents the different people in the workflow.

In this workflow lessons are identified by project staff, through after action reviews, retrospects or some other project-related mechanism. Early on it has to be decided whether this lesson is purely local. If so, the actions can be taken locally, local processes can be updated, and the lesson can be 'closed out' locally. If the lesson has an impact for other projects or parts of the organisation, then it is judged to be something that needs to be escalated to company level. Perhaps at this point the project manager gets involved to make sure that the lesson is well written and of good quality, and something that he or she is happy can be sent out on behalf of the project. The lesson is then submitted to a company

Figure 8.2 Example lesson flow

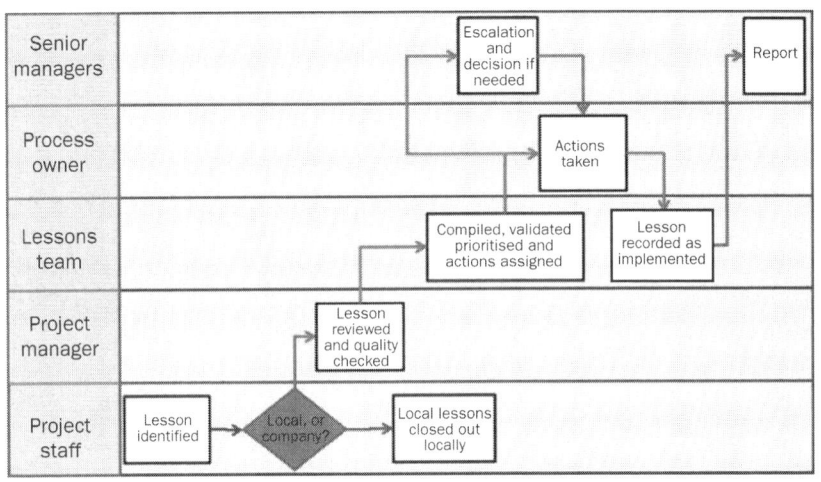

Senior managers			Escalation and decision if needed		Report
Process owner				Actions taken	
Lessons team			Compiled, validated prioritised and actions assigned	Lesson recorded as implemented	
Project manager			Lesson reviewed and quality checked		
Project staff	Lesson identified	Local, or company?	Local lessons closed out locally		

lessons learned database or a lessons learned team. Then the lesson is compared with other lessons, to see whether it is part of a trend. Staff validate the lesson, to make sure that it is true company-level learning rather than a local opinion. They may prioritise lessons into 'lessons for immediate action' or 'lessons for later review'. They may assign an action to the lesson (or this may have already been done at project level).

The next step is to forward the lesson to the process owner. If there is no lessons team, the process owner may themselves do the compilation, validation and prioritisation, and decide what action they need to take. If the process needs to be updated in any way, or if the process owner needs to take any other actions such as distributing the lesson or instigating any new training, then he or she takes that action, and the actions are recorded as having been implemented, and the lesson is 'closed'.

Sometimes deciding the action may not be straightforward. The action may be contentious, require additional spending, or need a fundamental change in the way that the company is operating. In a case like this, the lesson needs to be escalated to a senior level so that these big decisions can be taken. Also, if senior managers are interested in seeing how well the learning process is going, the lessons team (if there is one) may need to report to them regularly. This issue of reporting is covered in more detail in Chapter 12.

Validation and escalation

Somewhere in the learning process there needs to be at least one validation or quality control step. Somebody in the project may validate the lesson to make sure that it accurately reflects the learning that was discussed during the lesson identification process, and that the lesson is well written and contains enough context to be understood. This level of validation was covered in Chapter 6.

In addition to this step, somebody else may need to validate the actions assigned to the lesson, to make sure that processes really do need to be updated. This is done by either a central learning group, or by the process owners themselves. This second validation step seeks to answer the following questions:

- *Is this really a new lesson?* Quite often a lesson is identified when an existing process has not been followed, because the project team didn't know about the process, was using an old process, or for some other reason did not follow the existing process. In this case, no process update action is needed. Maybe the process owner needs to publicise the process a bit better, to make sure that everybody knows about it and is following it, but the process itself doesn't need to be updated.

- *Does the identified lesson really merit a process update?* Maybe there was some specific context associated with the lessons that will never be repeated. Maybe these circumstances will never happen again, and so the process really doesn't merit updating. Or maybe the lesson is more of an opinion than something that is learned. Perhaps it is an idea, rather than a fact derived from experience. The process owner needs to assess this and decide whether the evidence is sufficient to merit updating the process. Obviously it is going to be very difficult for the process owner to make this sort of validation judgement unless the lesson was particularly well written in the first place. That is partly why it is so important to ensure that lessons are written well.

- *Can the process be updated to incorporate this new learning, without causing an unacceptable increase in risk?* Updating a process or changing a process may improve performance, but may also bring risk. The process owner needs to understand the change well enough to know whether the new benefits it will bring will outweigh any additional risks. In some cases, especially with company standards or any processes that have safety and integrity implications, the process owner may need to go through a management of change process to make sure that the change can be carried out safely.

If the process owner can answer yes to the three questions above, then he or she needs to update the process based on the new learning. If the lesson was very well written, this may be enough for them to know what update is required. Otherwise, they may need to follow up with the originator of the lesson to gain more understanding and context.

Documenting processes

We have talked above about how the process owner needs to be involved in updating processes, and we still need to consider the issue of how the processes should be documented in the first place.

There is no single right way to do this, and different processes may need to be documented in different ways, but there are certain principles that you need to bear in mind when putting together any sort of guidance document for a process:

- *Make it clear how optional any particular process is*. Processes can be more or less optional, and this must be covered in the documentation. In BP drilling in the late 1990s, corporate process documentation was divided into three categories: principles, processes and practices. The labelling of these made it very clear to the reader how much scope they had to vary the process from what was in the documentation. These are the three main levels of optionality:
    - *mandatory, or 'must do'*. This is the level of company standards, and everybody reading this particular process documentation needs to understand that they need to follow exactly what is written. If there is a major problem with applying what is written, they need to get in touch with the process owner and discuss it with them, but the default should be to follow this documentation exactly.
    - *advisory, or 'should do'*. This is the level of best practice, and everybody reading this particular process documentation needs to be clear that this is the best way to approach this particular process, based on current company knowledge. However, there is always the possibility to improve on best practice, and if somebody can find an even better way, then that's great. So use of the advisory process is advised, but not compulsory. However, if people ignore advisory knowledge and things go wrong, some awkward questions may be asked.

– *suggested, or 'could do'*. This is the level of good ideas or good practices that others in the organisation have used, which the reader should feel free to reuse or readapt to his or her own context. These good ideas can still save the reader a lot of time and effort, but there is no real requirement to copy them.

- *Document the process with the reader in mind.* The documentation needs to be focused on the person who has to apply the process, and to be packaged in such a way that they will find the documentation easy to follow and use. Make sure you include everything that the customer needs to be aware of, whether they know they need it or not. Consider what new users need to find if they are trying to follow the process documentation for the first time. First, they would like advice and recommendations on what to do, what not to do, and how and when to do it. Second, they would like some context. They would like to know how much they can trust the knowledge that they are offered, where it comes from, and who to speak to if they need more. To make process documentation really user-friendly and user-focused requires thought and effort by the process owner, but far less thought and effort from the person who needs to follow the documentation.

- *Remember that readers may not want all the detail all at once.* Quite often it is useful to give them an overview or a checklist, and then allow them to dive down into more detail as and when required. Several of the most successful process guides have a high-level summary, then sections with far more detail, including links to documents, videos, case studies and so on. Try and present the material in the most user-friendly way you can. For example, a thick manual is nowhere near as daunting when broken down into a linked series of online hypertext pages, and a dense page of instructions will be much more easy for the reader to understand if it is broken down into a series of frequently asked questions. FAQs are one of my preferred formats for documented best practices and process guidance as they are intuitively easy for readers to follow and can easily be updated. Checklists are another preferred format, which can be a very powerful way to convey a series of process steps.

- *Use multimedia.* There are some types of knowledge which are easier to convey in photographs or through video. Your process guides do not need to be purely text-based. Don't tell if you can show.

- *Store the process guides somewhere that users will find them.* Put them on the intranet, the corporate file server, in shared space, and make sure that they can be easily searched and located. Make them search engine friendly. Make sure that the relevant search terms are in the document titles, document tags and metatags, and in headlines within the documents. Make sure that they have a title that will be relevant to the person seeking them.

- *Include relevant metadata.* The process guidance documents should carry the name of the process owner and the date of the last update. In some industries a 'valid until' date is also included.

Once the process documents have been written, or updated based on new lessons, then we could be forgiven for assuming that the improved processes will be followed in future, and that improved performance will result. However, this will not happen if people in the organisation are unaware that processes have been updated, and so continue to follow old practices. Nor will it happen if people ignore the processes. In the next chapter, we will look at ways of broadcasting new knowledge, to ensure that the lessons will be reused.

9

Ensuring lessons and updated processes are re-applied

In the previous chapters we discussed how lessons can be identified from activity, how actions can be assigned to those lessons, how the actions may often be for a process owner to update a process, and how a process owner may review, validate and act on the lessons. However, even if this part of the learning loop works perfectly and lessons are routinely taken forward into improved processes, this still won't have an impact on performance unless people across the organisation start to apply those improved processes in business activity.

To make sure that this happens, we need to address a couple of factors: make sure people are notified of any process improvements, and that they can refer to, review and internalise improved process before taking action. So there are a number of items we need to address in this chapter, including:

- broadcasting new lessons and improved processes
- feeding improved processes into training
- including process review within the work process.

Broadcasting new lessons and process improvements

We talked in the previous chapter about the process owner's accountability for making sure that processes are well defined and well documented. A second accountability for the process owner is to make sure that the community of process users is kept notified of any process updates. The process owner can do this in several ways:

- *by publishing a blog*, to keep people updated with all changes and new lessons related to the process that they own. The process owner needs to ensure that everyone who needs to be notified is copied into the blog, and then it can be an excellent way of broadcasting. Not only will the notifications come via email (and everyone reads email), the blog itself will provide a searchable record of all changes. Through comments to the blog, the process owner can enter into discussion with process users and clarify any points that are unclear. For example, in SABMiller, the head of information security publishes a regular blog with information security announcements and updates to information security processes.

- *by publishing a newsletter*, which is in many ways the print version of a blog. In some companies print is still preferred to electronic media (even though it is more difficult to search a newsletter, and impossible to discuss items on a newsletter in the way that you can on a blog). In BP Drilling, a regular newsletter called 'Well Connected' is used to distribute new lessons, new knowledge and new processes.

- *by using a community of practice discussion forum*, which has the advantage that all the members of the community are (or should be) subscribed to the forum, and that it is very easy then for people to comment on the process improvements or new lessons. In Conoco Phillips, each community works through software that incorporates a Q&A forum and a notification forum for new lessons and new ideas.

- *by using an email distribution list*, but this is probably the least satisfactory method, as there is then no place for community discussion, comments or feedback.

- *by using RSS feeds* from the process documentation to notify the user community of any changes. SharePoint also has a notification mechanism, which can be used to notify people of process documentation updates.

- *by using proprietary software*; for example, Ford used web-hosted software called the Ford Best Practice Replication system to replicate and leverage quality improvement practices across the organisation. Lessons and process improvements identified in one manufacturing site were distributed automatically to the other sites for review and for action. The software also included the facility to record what each site had done as a result of this notification, the process improvement and how much it had saved them in operating or production costs (see further details in Chapter 10).

Process improvements and training

Training is one of the most effective ways of helping people to interact with, and so internalise, new knowledge and improved processes. Many organisations are now looking at training as being just one component of a learning organisation, and as part of a holistic system for learning, involving communities of practice, on-the-job learning activities (such as some of the ones we have discussed), e-learning and traditional off-the-job training.

If training is to be effective as a way of helping people internalise improved processes, people need to be trained in the processes at the point that they need them. Training is most effective when participants have an immediate need to use what they have learned. The link between process improvement and training is probably closest in the military sector. In the US Army and UK Army the development of process (known to the military as 'doctrine'), and training personnel in the new processes, are both covered by the same part of the organisation, known as TRADOC (training and doctrine command). This is a description of the US TRADOC (*http://www.army.mil/info/organization/unitsandcommands/commandstructure/tradoc/*):

> TRADOC develops the Army's Soldiers and Civilian leaders and designs, develops and integrates capabilities, concepts and doctrine in order to build a campaign-capable, expeditionary Army in support of joint warfighting capability.

'Designs, develops and integrates' is an excellent summary of how this group operates as part of the learning cycle. TRADOC acts as a process owner for the doctrine, and ensures that the relevant people are trained in the doctrines they need. This close coupling between process ownership and training allows updated doctrines to be carried forward immediately into updated training material.

However, the use of training in the armed forces is exceptional compared with training in commercial organisations. In the military, it is quite common for 30 per cent of the budget to be spent on training, and training is required for all troops before they are deployed to operations. In industry, the training budget is usually much less than this, formal training tends to be divorced from the business cycle, and there may be a significant interval between employees being trained and them actually using the material discussed in the training. Nevertheless, it is equally important that people are trained in updated processes. Therefore there needs to be a link between process owners and trainers to allow new content to feed through into the training curriculum.

Process review as part of operations

Although training in industry is not as much a natural part of the operational cycle as it is in the military, many organisations conduct some sort of regular process review during operations, and this provides an opportunity to introduce updated processes. These process reviews can include peer review, before action review and knowledge management planning.

Peer review

Peer review is a process used in many projects as a periodic check on the quality of work before making further commitment to proceed. The project manager hosts a meeting, and invites other managers, technical authorities and subject matter experts to review the work to date. They can bring their up-to-date knowledge of current processes to see whether anything has been missed by the project team, and give them any tips and hints about the next stages of the project. The main problem with peer review is that the meetings are usually held after the event, as the work has to have been done in order for the peers to review it. This has led many companies to introduce the additional process of peer assist, which will be described in more detail in Chapter 11.

Before action review

Before action review is a process used by teams to prepare for upcoming activities, and to align objectives and make plans. Completing a before action review not only focuses intent, but also gives the opportunity to discuss any potential problems and lessons learned from previous actions, and to look for process updates. The before action review involves asking the following questions:

- What are the intended results?
- What challenges can we anticipate?
- What has been learned from similar situations?
- What processes do we need to follow, and have any of these been updated?
- How can we improve on previous experiences?

Similar pre-activity meetings may be known as toolbox talks or pre-shift meetings.

Technical limits

In the oil drilling sector, Shell conducts a detailed form of before action review and planning, known as a technical limit meeting. This is a combination of learning from the past (the planning is based on a thorough understanding of past performance and past lessons), tacit knowledge exchange (the operational crews bring their detailed knowledge to the event) and innovation (the driver for the meeting is to innovate beyond the best of past performance).

The concept is relatively simple. It involves using the knowledge and experience of the drilling crews in perfecting the drilling execution plan. In the past, the oil company would prepare the drilling plan, which would be passed to the drilling contractor, who would drill the well. However, the drilling crews (the staff who actually do the work) are usually the people who know best how the work can be done, and are familiar with the lessons from previous wells. So by involving them during detailed planning, the oil companies can not only access the lessons and build a better plan, but also involve the drilling crews in setting and adopting aggressive performance targets.

The technical limit process consists of the following stages:

- An engagement exercise is conducted so that the project team, project manager, customer and contractors all buy in to the use of the process.
- The project team, project manager and customer agree the primary performance indicator for the project.
- The project team divides the project plan into the smallest possible component activities and tasks. For example, the drilling plan may be divided into several hundred steps, each of which will take between half an hour and a day to complete.
- The project team collects performance data on all of these steps. The team is looking to find the best and the average performance for each step.
- This detailed breakdown of activity and performance is presented at a technical limit meeting.
- The meeting breaks into small groups who go through the plan step by step. For each step they ask questions in three areas:
  - 'Do we need to do this step?'
  - 'If we do need to do it, can we take it off the critical path?'

- 'If this step is on the critical path, how can we do it as quickly as possible? What needs to be in place to deliver best performance? What lessons are available?'
- They also look at the risks involved with any changes to the programme, and set a target time for each step. This should be at least as quick as the best historical performance.
- This revised plan and revised performance targets are then put into action, and reviewed daily.

Typically a drilling team may find they can save 10–20 per cent of operational time by taking tasks off the critical path or by eliminating them altogether, and an additional 10–20 per cent operational time by optimising the tasks that remain based on lessons from the past.

Knowledge management planning

Knowledge management planning takes place in the early stages of a project, around the same time that the risk management planning, operational planning, manpower planning and so on are being carried out. The project team members attend a knowledge management planning workshop, where they identify the crucial knowledge they will need to deliver the project. For each of these critical knowledge areas they discuss where to find the knowledge they need, who they need to speak to, what actions need to be taken to acquire the knowledge, and the person who will take the action.

The sources of knowledge are very often the documented processes, the subject matter experts and the process owners. Therefore, as part of the process, project team members commit to the action of finding and reviewing the most recent versions of the relevant processes, and any additional lessons learned that may be relevant to the project. Knowledge management planning therefore coordinates, plans and assigns accountability for learning in the early stages of the project. Provided the updated processes are easily accessible and easily followed, the learning loop is closed.

Scenario planning

Scenario planning can also be used as a thinking tool before embarking on major decisions. Here a number of 'what if' events or drivers are brainstormed, the critical factors and 'game changing' possibilities are selected, and a small group of future scenarios are created. Each of these is then written up and used as a basis for testing strategies. Lessons learned from the past can be used to ensure that the strategic response to each scenario is viable.

Through pre-activity review, training and broadcast of updated processes, and by ensuring that the updated processes are easily found and understood, there is a good chance that the lessons identified from an activity will be carried through to future activities, and that performance will improve as a result.

10

Technology to support lesson learning

So far in this book we have been looking at the processes associated with learning lessons, with updating corporate process documentation, and with applying those updated processes into future action. We have also talked about some of the accountabilities involved, especially those involved with the process ownership. Technology has a role to play in the lesson learning cycle as well, and the learning loop shown in Figure 10.1 shows three areas where technology has a crucial role to play:

- to host the repository for lessons, allowing them to be recorded in a standard form, to be searched and retrieved, for actions to be assigned, and for the status of individual lessons to be tracked; this repository often takes the form of a lessons learned database
- to host the knowledge library, which forms a repository for the process documents of the organisation
- to provide search software and publish software, which allows updated processes to be sought by people, and 'pushed' to those who need to be notified.

We will look at these areas of technology one by one.

Lesson repositories

If lessons are being identified from many projects, for example from retrospects and after action reviews, then these lessons need to be collected and stored somewhere where they can be compared, reconciled and the actions assigned. They need to be recorded in a consistent format and stored in a central system, which is often some sort of lessons learned database. Lessons learned databases can be set up for a single project, to store and track the lessons from within the project, or for the entire organisation, to store and track lessons from many projects.

Figure 10.1 Technology and the learning loop

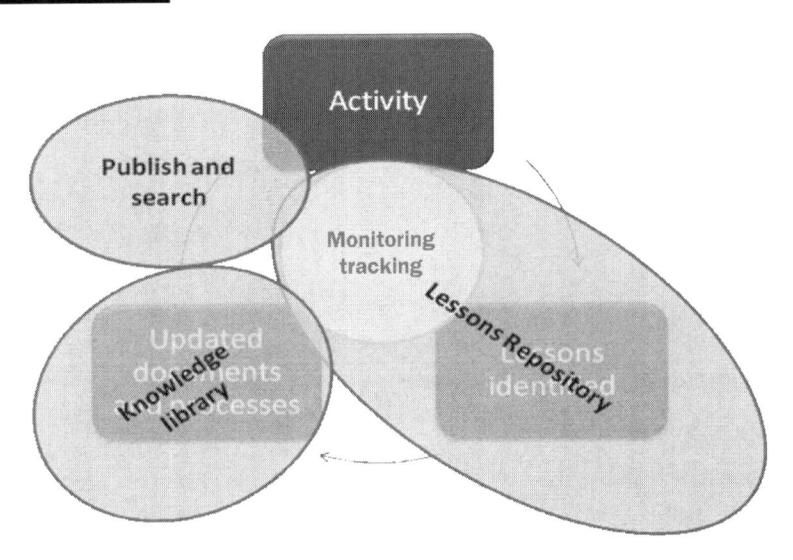

Lessons learned databases are a common component of company-wide knowledge management systems, and many examples of such databases can be found on the World Wide Web. Unfortunately, they can often suffer from bad structure and/or unhelpful content. If you intend to put together a lessons learned database, the advice below will help you produce something that can help deliver sustainable business performance improvement. Also bear in mind that discipline and patience is required to fill in a database properly, which can be a barrier (see also Chapter 15).

Store single lessons in a process-based taxonomy

An effective lessons learned database should be structured according to the needs of the 'knowledge user'. People who access lessons from the database should be able to find what they are looking for very easily. If they don't find relevant and useful knowledge within a few minutes, they will leave and never come back. Think about the needs and interests of the knowledge user, how the knowledge will be reused, and how you should structure the database to give users easy access to what they need.

A common mistake is to structure the database according to how the knowledge was supplied. The lessons might be grouped by project, for example, with all the lessons from a single project being grouped together (sometimes even grouped together in a single document). However, this is of little use to the person who is looking for the lessons. They don't necessarily know the history of previous projects, or what has been learned on which projects; they are more likely to want to find all the lessons to do with a specific activity. They may be looking for lessons about procuring steel pipe, or for all the lessons to do with safety while working at height, or for all the lessons to do with partnering with a particular national authority; in other words, lessons to do with the particular issue that they face.

The lessons therefore need to be grouped into a structure, index or taxonomy based on work activity or work process. We talked in Chapter 8 about process ownership, and if there's an existing structure of process ownership, then the taxonomy in the lessons database should follow this. If there's no existing taxonomy, then you have to get together with some of the functional experts in your organisation and build one. Make it simple; don't make it more than two layers deep.

Use a common structure for lessons

In Chapter 5 we talked about how lessons should be written down; how they should be specific and actionable; how they should be expressed as recommendations; how they should contain context and background; and how they should be associated with certain metadata. Figure 10.2 shows a typical structure for a lessons database entry.

This contains five text fields for describing the lesson, and a series of additional fields for metadata. The text fields include:

- context
- description of the event
- root cause
- lessons identified
- suggested action.

When lessons are identified through a retrospect or after action review, you will find that the structure shown in Figure 10.2 follows the discussion that will have happened during lesson identification. The five questions of the after action review, described in Chapter 5, correspond completely to these five text fields.

In addition to the five text fields, we have the metadata fields such as the lesson title, originator and date. The fields for topic and sub-topic represent the process-based taxonomy that we discussed above, and the other fields have already been discussed in Chapter 5. An example of a

The Lessons Learned Handbook

Figure 10.2 Typical format for a lesson database entry form

Field	What you need to input
Lesson title	Short sentence
Lesson ID number	Assigned automatically
Submitted by	Name, role, department of originator
Date submitted	dd/mm/yyyy
Status	Submitted/approved/implemented
Topic	From taxonomy
Sub-topic	From taxonomy
Project name	Project name
Context	The context in which this learning happened – any relevant background
Description of the event	What actually happened?
Root cause	What were the root causes?
Lesson identified	The recommendations for the future – specific actionable recommendation
Suggested action	How can these recommendations be institutionalised? For example, update a process, write a process, fix a problem, notify a person
Accountable person	Name, role, department
Action approval date	dd/mm/yyyy
Closure date	dd/mm/yyyy
Lesson value	If possible
Other comments and attachments	

completed lesson is shown in Figure 10.3, for the example lesson within a refinery unit from Chapter 5 (Case Study 5.2), using pseudonyms.

The advantage of having a template such as this one for submitting lessons is that it will prompt the person who is entering the data to think hard about what advice they want to give to the knowledge user, and about how they should categorise the lesson so that it can be found easily. After that, data entry is largely a question of selecting options and filling in boxes (even though there is no guarantee that this will ensure quality data input).

Technology to support lesson learning

Figure 10.3 Example of a completed lesson

Field	What you need to input
Lesson title	Tray and weir installation
Lesson ID number	1227538
Submitted by	L J Yung
Date submitted	12/09/2008
Status	Submitted pending approval
Topic	Maintenance shutdown
Sub-topic	Fractionating columns
Project name	Kuala Lumpur refinery, plant shutdown, 2008
Context	We were supposed: • to install trays, with weir heights and downcomers within tolerance • to hold tray assembly in place with appropriate hardware, e.g. bolts and nuts, clamps, washers, slide fasteners, etc.
Description of the event	1. Tray clearances were not within tolerance. 2. There was a shortage of hardware.
Root cause	1. Workers were using measuring tapes to adjust the clearances resulting in a need for repeated re-working. 2. Workers were transporting the hardware up the column in bulk, resulting in hardware being missplaced, dropped, or not following vendor's instruction on the appropriate type of hardware to be used.
Lesson identified	1. Use standard blocks prepared to the required dimensions for adjusting weir height and downcomer clearance. 2. Put all the appropriate hardware in place on the tray sections at ground level before transporting up the column.
Suggested action	1. Request the workshop to construct a series of standard blocks. 2. Update daily orders for tray installation.
Accountable person	1. Workshop supervisor 2. Works manager
Action approval date	20/09/2008
Closure date	20/10/2008
Lesson value	$5000
Other comments and attachments	[diagram showing dimensions of standard blocks]

Metadata

There are other items that you will probably want to document as part of the identified lesson, for example:

- *Lesson title.* Give the lesson a sensible title, as many times when people search for lessons, the title is the first thing they see. So you need to give it a title which lets people know what they found, such as 'improved process for steam-cleaning wall tiles' or 'project costing; lessons from a failed bid for insurance provision to General Motors'. Don't call it 'lesson number 35', 'failure analysis' or 'learnings from the Tiger project'; none of these titles tell you anything about the nature of the lesson itself.

- *Topic and sub-topic.* These will come from the taxonomy, and should be pre-entered (chosen from a pull-down list) so people find it easy to select a valid choice.

- *Originator.* Somebody will have identified the lesson, and will have first-hand experience of its details. Record their name as the originator of the lesson. This does two things: it gives people somebody to contact if they want more detail, and it provides recognition of the initiative and efforts of the originator in identifying the lesson. Sometimes the learning historian or a facilitator will write the lessons, and they may need to be identified as well, if only to take the blame if the lesson is badly written.

- *Date of the event, date of identification of the lesson, and/or date of documentation.* If you are going to record all three of these dates, then ideally they should be as close together as possible. Certainly one of the three dates should be recorded, so the reader can know how old the lesson is, and the organisation can track how long it takes to close out lessons.

- *Action.* We covered the assignment of actions to lessons in Chapter 7.

- *Lesson classification.* In some cases you may need to classify whether this is a company confidential lesson, a top secret lesson, or it has open and unrestricted distribution. This is particularly important in military or intelligence lesson-learning systems, where there are many degrees of security classification.

- *Lesson status.* It may be a draft lesson, it may be validated, the actions may be open, or the actions may have been completed and therefore the whole lesson may be closed.

- *Lesson value*. Where possible, it might be useful to put an estimate of value on the lessons. This will either be the financial (or other) impact from the particular problem or mistake that prompted the identification of the lesson, or the estimated financial (or other) impact that the process improvement is estimated to deliver. This value is a lot easier to assign where performance is managed closely; Ford, with the wealth of metrics on its manufacturing process, was able to assign a value to every performance improvement. If it is not possible to assign a dollar value, then you can use value judgements such as minor, medium, significant or critical. This helps others sort and rank lessons in the database more easily.

Use pictures

In transferring knowledge, as in so many other applications, a picture is worth a thousand words. A lessons learned database that transfers lessons only in text misses a huge opportunity. The originator of the lessons should be able to attach photographs, diagrams, audio recordings or video files, whatever he or she needs in order to demonstrate the lesson. For example, in offshore operations nowadays the drilling crew will frequently keep a digital camera handy, and photograph equipment before and after it is used. Whether operations go well or badly, the photographic record can often be very valuable in transferring knowledge to other teams. In a construction setting, it may be very useful to have photographs taken during construction, or it might be useful to be able to attach engineering drawings to the lessons database. In a consulting organisation, it may be very useful to attach PowerPoint slidesets from successful pitches to clients. Databases of safety lessons in particular should be set up to allow photographs to be attached, as photographs of accidents and near misses can be extremely powerful ways of alerting others about danger and risk.

Allow push and search

One of the biggest hurdles in any knowledge management system is getting people to look for knowledge, advice and lessons. No matter how well structured and searchable the lessons learned database may be, this will not help if people don't go to the database in the first place.

However it may be possible to set up a 'push database', which will forward lessons to interested parties, rather than requiring them to go and search. SharePoint, for example, allows individuals to subscribe to be notified of new items, and this functionality allows lessons to be forwarded to people with an interest in a particular topic. Case Study 10.1, reprinted from Gorelick, Milton and April (2004), shows the power of this notification.

Case Study 10.1 The BP Valhall platform in the Norwegian North Sea

On the BP Valhall platform in the Norwegian North Sea, the wells team had developed an innovative method of widening the wellbore on extended reach wells by running a tool called a Near Bit Reamer behind the rotary steerable drilling assembly. Where previously they would have pulled out the drillstring, put on a new bottom hole assembly, and drilled a 'hole opening run' to widen the hole, they were now able to do this in one operation, so saving between three and five days of rig time. At the end-of-well retrospect this was identified as new knowledge, and Marton Haga, the drilling engineer, was tasked with entering details into the LINK lessons database. LINK automatically forwarded the lesson to other teams working on extended reach wells, one of which was the team working in Trinidad. This team was intrigued by the approach, and contacted Marton for more information. He was more than happy to help, and sent details of procedures and reference runs. The Trinidad team assessed the possibilities, decided this was a valuable approach, and invited Marton to a peer assist to share his operational knowledge. The technique was applied during the 2000 drilling season in Trinidad resulting in a $900,000 cost saving. The Trinidad team refined the process slightly, and has shared its new knowledge with the rest of the community through articles in the newsletter 'Well Connected' (and lessons in LINK).

Technology to support lesson learning

The most important person to push the lesson to is whoever is accountable for taking action as a result, whether this is a process owner accountable for updating of process, or somebody accountable for fixing a problem. It should be relatively straightforward to set up the database so that it sends a notification to this accountable person, by email or via an RSS feed. The process owner should certainly be notified about any lessons related to his or her specific process, whether they have any actions to take or not.

In addition, the database should be searchable. Searches should be possible on many fields, as well as through free text. Ideally the free text search should be semi-intelligent, and should compensate for different spellings and descriptions of the same thing. For example, in a global organisation a search for 'vapour detection systems' should also return items about 'vapor detection systems'. Also people can search for pending lessons for which they are accountable, to remind themselves of actions they need to take. Or the lesson learning coordinator can search to find out how many lessons are pending, how many are completed, and how many are awaiting validation. The lessons database then becomes a source of tracking metrics, to track the usage of the learning system.

Knowledge libraries

The second key area of technology is the knowledge library. This represents the structured repository for process documentation and guidance. There are a number of possibilities for technology to support a knowledge library. The simplest is a shared file structure; this is either a set of folders on the drive, or a set of files within a SharePoint site. More complex than this, but far more easy to browse and use, is a portal. The third option is a wiki.

Knowledge portals

Most companies have a web-based system or portal for structuring and storing internal knowledge, so that it can be accessed through a web browser. Corporate intranets became more popular as organisations started to realise that they could provide a simple route, via a web browser, to a library of company information and explicit knowledge. As the demand for the provision of portals grew, so too did the tools that

111

the IT department could use to create and management content. Today it is not unusual for company employees to be able to publish direct to the company portal and portals are becoming more and more customised to the needs of individual users. Portals have also been seen as the way of integrating legacy applications in organisations, a situation which frequently occurs when one organisation is acquired by another.

Process owners within an organisation find portals an extremely useful way of structuring process documentation, and making it browsable and searchable. As discussed in Chapter 8, the level of validity of the documentation can also be made very visible. For example, Young (2007) explains how the BP Operations Excellence toolkit was structured around the level of validation that has been applied to the knowledge (see Case Study 10.2).

Case Study 10.2 The BP Operations Excellence toolkit

The BP Operations Excellence toolkit is structured around the level of validation that has been applied to the knowledge. At one level there is the highly vetted, approved knowledge in the form of corporate standards and required practices, which are referenced under the heading 'The BP Way'. At the opposite end of the spectrum is the knowledge in the question and response system, eCLIPS, which is totally unvetted. BP went a step further and provided a 'health guide' to the advice you were receiving.

Captured knowledge is presented in a hierarchy:

- *'The BP Way'*: These tools describe the way BP does business (BP policy). This should be the first place to look when identifying ways (the 'what' and 'how').

- *Good practices*: These describe good practices for work processes, identified either by experience from operating assets (e.g. assessments or community discussions) or by subject matter experts.

- *People*: These are people you can contact for help with closing gaps identified in the internal benchmarking process.

Technology to support lesson learning

- *Communities*: These are communities of practice related to specific work practices.

- *eCLIPS community discussion forum*: This section links you to any questions (and responses) that have been asked about specific work practices, and allows you to ask the community if you have been unable to find an answer in the toolkit. All entries in eCLIPS are purely voluntary and are not validated by subject matter experts. Community Q&A tools of this sort are described in Chapter 9.

This hierarchy is very important as it gives the reader a sense of how reliable the knowledge might be. Thus if the advice provided is in the form of 'the BP Way' then the reader knows that this is a fully validated and approved policy or procedure and can be followed with confidence. At the bottom end of the scale, advice provided via the eCLIPS system, which is not validated, needs to be treated with a lot more caution.

One problem with portals is that it can often be very difficult to add content to them. For well-established and mature processes, this is not a problem, as content will be only rarely be added or updated. However, for process knowledge that is dynamically evolving, it can be extremely useful to allow readers to comment on the documentation, or even to edit it, as new lessons are learned and new knowledge becomes available. This is where wikis can add huge value.

Wikis

A wiki is a website that allows staff to edit, add and delete content. These collaborative tools initially found favour among groups that were jointly creating complex documents such as standards and manuals. However, as the technology has evolved, and the ease of use of the wiki sites increased, they have started to be used to retain corporate best practice in a form that allows it to be annotated by others. For example, engineers in one manufacturing company are using a wiki to store and share knowledge about the operation and maintenance of conveyor belts. In another

113

example, an oil company is using the knowledge of experienced operators to build a wiki on the subject of bitumen production. Bitumen production is a tricky process, which requires considerable operator experience. This latter wiki is being updated from the results of learning interviews.

Shell makes extensive use of a wiki as a corporate knowledge base (see Hendrix, 2007). The Shell wiki was launched in 2006, to provide access to operational business know-how as well as to general knowledge on the Shell organisation, and to make available training material from the Shell University. The content of the wiki was originally created by subject matter experts, but the articles are open to comment by readers, and will be updated if these comments identify new lessons or other process improvements.

A good way of getting started with wikis is to put the current practice, or the current 'way of doing something', onto the site, and ask staff to contribute their experience and ideas on how to improve it. Through this process, it is possible to tap rapidly into a wide range of experience. Once the experiences have been shared and best practice developed, this should be taken off the wiki site and put somewhere more permanent.

Wikis are often assumed to involve informal, bottom-up submission of material designed to draw on the wisdom of crowds. The often quoted example is Wikipedia, which has no formal content-ownership roles (though the editorial roles are becoming far stronger), but instead relies on voluntary ad hoc submission and edits by the readership. However, the major drawback of the Wikipedia model is that it requires a huge user base. There is a much-published rule applied to voluntary wikis, the 1:9:90 rule. This states that for any one wiki, the majority of content will come from 1 per cent of the user base; a further 9 per cent will add some, more minor, content; and 90 per cent of users will never contribute at all. So if we look at the potential knowledge contribution from the members:

- 1 per cent will contribute 100 per cent of their knowledge.
- 9 per cent will contribute (say) 10 per cent of their knowledge.
- 90 per cent will contribute nothing.

The voluntarily populated wiki will therefore only access about 2 per cent of the knowledge of the user base, leaving the wisdom of 98 per cent of the crowd untapped.

Many organisations overcome this by assigning accountabilities for wiki entry. In Chapter 15, Peter Kemper describes how lessons from incident investigations (which have been the subject of formal learning investigations) can be used as a routine feed to wiki content. The wiki in this case acts as an unstructured lessons database, strengthened even further by providing a back office service that creates the necessary links to ensure that new knowledge and new lessons are fully linked to the rest of the wiki.

Publish and search technology

As explained in the previous chapter, updated processes and new lessons may need to be broadcast around the organisation, so that people starting activity can find, or will be notified of, any process improvements. Again, technology can be a huge help.

Search engines

Any knowledge library needs a good search engine. There are many options for enterprise search, and there are few organisations now without good search functionality.

Blogs

A blog is an online journal, published on the internet or intranet, where an individual (or potentially a team) keeps a public diary of text and graphics. The issue of validation is crucial, if blogs are to be used as part of a learning system. Most blogs on the internet contain opinion, rather than validated knowledge. However, in an operational knowledge management setting, blogs are an excellent mechanism for a process owner, a subject matter expert or a community of practice leader, to notify the organisation of new lessons, and updated and improved processes.

RSS feeds

RSS (really simple syndication) is a way for people to subscribe to relevant blogs, databases, portals and websites, in order to be notified of any new content. New lessons and process improvements can be automatically forwarded to your RSS reader as soon as they are published, without you needing to browse the websites. Each individual may need to download an RSS reader to their computer, and then visit the websites and blogs they wish to subscribe to, but many organisations provide these as a standard tool, and anyone who uses Microsoft Outlook 2007 will find that it can be used as a perfectly acceptable RSS reader.

The process owners and subject matter experts need to set up their sites and blogs to provide RSS feeds. More and more tools these days are provided with RSS feed capabilities built in. Sharepoint 2007 has this capability as an embedded default, for example.

Tagging

Tagging provides an alternative option to a built-in taxonomy for indexing a lessons database. The benefit of a taxonomy, and the weakness of a taxonomy, is its rigidity. Allowing content providers to tag lessons with the most likely terms, and then allowing customers to apply their own tags, can provide a more dynamic method of providing access to lessons in a way that truly relates to the needs of the users, provided of course that the system allows for tag-based queries.

References

Gorelick, C., Milton, N. and April, K. (eds) (2004) *Performance Through Learning: Knowledge Management in Practice*, Elsevier.

Hendrix, D. (2007) Focusing on behaviors and learning at Shell, *Knowledge Management Review*, July/August.

Young, T. (2007) *Knowledge Management for Services, Operations and Manufacturing*, Chandos.

11

Sharing and seeking the unwritten lessons

So far this book has been describing a formal, deliberate and systematic process for identifying, documenting and acting upon lessons, for updating company processes and procedures, and for carrying these forward into action. A system like this, with its clear accountabilities and ability for lessons to be tracked through to closure, is very important for any organisation that wishes to institutionalise the method for continuous performance improvement.

However, this is not the only way lessons are shared, as discussed in Chapter 3. The lessons learned system we have described is what you might call a 'push' loop, because the lessons are 'pushed' out into the organisation by the originator. It also might be described as a 'collect' loop, in that the lessons are 'collected' and made explicit or written down, and therefore transferred in written form. It is also formal, and can be metricated and reported against. However, very many lessons will never be written down nor find their way into any database or process guidance documentation. You could call these 'tacit' lessons, and the transfer of these lessons will be by 'connect' – by connecting people so they can discuss the learning. In knowledge management, the terms 'tacit' and 'explicit' are often used to describe the knowledge that is held in people's heads and the knowledge that is recorded or written down.

The transfer of lessons from person to person can also be driven by 'pull' – by people asking for lessons, and asking what others have learnt about a specific topic. We can distinguish between 'knowledge push' (people proactively sharing what they know with the others) and 'knowledge pull' (people proactively asking others to share what they know). Finally, as discussed in Chapter 3, there can be varying degrees of formality in the learning approach.

Therefore, in addition to the systematic learning loop that we have described, organisations should put in place structures and mechanisms that allow people to seek lessons beyond those which they know they will already find in the lessons database, and which allow people to discuss lessons that may never have been collected and recorded. Several structures and processes are described in this chapter, including:

- communities of practice
- peer assist
- baton passing
- knowledge handover
- promoting conversation.

I am not intending to discuss the ad hoc lesson sharing that goes on in social networks. For me, learning lessons is too important to be ad hoc and social networking, although acting as an agent for culture change, needs to be supplemented by business networking.

Several of these methods of tacit knowledge sharing, such as peer assist, and the use of communities of practice, can be seen in the description of lesson learning at Mars, Inc, in Chapter 14.

Communities of practice

Communities of practice are peer networks of practitioners within an organisation, who help each other perform better by sharing lessons and knowledge. For example, a community of practice might be set up for electrical engineers, so that engineers can raise issues and problems, and see if anyone in the community can provide insights and suggest solutions. Many of the larger companies have set up dozens of communities of practice, some of which may have over a thousand members. Communities generally have a facilitator or moderator, and may sometimes have a sophisticated governance system. Community members exchange knowledge in two ways: by capturing and sharing process documents, or by using a Q&A forum to ask each other for help and advice.

We introduced the concept of communities of practice in Chapter 8, because community leaders may often play the role of process owner. However, there may be very many process users in a community of practice, and many of them may have lessons and experience which they have never written down. An engineering community of practice, for example, may contain process users for rotating machinery, for instrumentation and control, for electrical engineering and so on. The community of practice therefore not only helps to create the process documentation and best practices, but also collectively holds a collection of unwritten lessons in the heads of its members.

For a community of practice to operate effectively as a mechanism for sharing unwritten lessons, it needs the following enablers.

Asking questions and giving answers

The primary way for community members to access the unwritten lessons is by asking questions. Any community member facing a problem in their project where they lack complete knowledge should have a means of asking the community for help, and of receiving answers. In a colocated community, this can be done in regular face-to-face meetings. For example, the communities of practice ('tech clubs') in the Chrysler Auburn Hill plant in the 1990s met weekly or fortnightly to solve problems and exchange good practices. An engineer working on brake systems for jeeps may have a problem, which he could raise at the 'Braking Systems' tech club, and receive answers from people working on braking systems in vans, small cars, and so on.

Communities of practice in dispersed or multinational businesses cannot meet regularly in person. They need some virtual means of raising questions and receiving answers. There are very many web-based or email-based discussion forums, or Q&A forum tools, that allow just this facility, and these are proven and popular tools for sharing knowledge within communities. The World Bank, for example, operates several global communities of practice, each with its own Q&A forum, so that field workers anywhere in the world can access lessons from their peers by sending an email asking for lessons and advice. Questions will be forwarded to all members of the community by email, and anybody who can share their learning will reply. Replies are collated as a 'threaded discussion' on a community forum, which community members can read and learn from.

A sense of identity

The members of a community are happy to share lessons with each other because they feel a sense of identity with each other. They see each other as fellow practitioners, sharing the same challenges and difficulties, and having valuable learning to share. People will feel 'at home' in a community if they identify with the community topic and community members. Therefore the most effective communities tend to be the ones that deal with people's professions. In Shell, some of the most effective communities are those of geologists and geophysicists: people with a specialist discipline, who work full time in the discipline, speak a specific technical language, identify with the topic, and have a passion for the subject. When you get a group of geologists in a bar, they tend to talk geology all night. This is the sort of professional interest, energy and identification with the topic that will really hold a community together. The sense of identity can be strengthened through regular face-to-face meetings of the community.

An energetic coordinator

The community of practice needs a defined coordinator to be accountable for the smooth operation of the community. Responsibilities of the coordinator include:

- managing the community discussions (online and face to face)
- making sure agreed community behaviours are followed
- setting up the community meetings
- working with the community core team
- liaising with subject matter experts and process owners
- watching for problems where knowledge sharing is not happening
- maintaining the membership list
- representing the community to management
- managing the lifecycle of the community
- keeping energy levels high among participants, to ensure active participation.

The community coordinator is not necessarily a process owner, and does not need to be a technical authority. The most important attributes for the community coordinator are passion and energy. Community coordinators act as dynamos for the community, keeping energy levels high and positive. They need to be insiders, members of the organisation, well known and well respected, and practitioners in the topic. They have to understand the jargon and the language, and to know the key players. The community leaders can be appointed (as in Buckman laboratories), be nominated by the community (as in Shell), or emerge as natural leaders based on their passion and energy (as in some BP communities). They can be called coordinators, facilitators, leaders or minders, whatever terminology is acceptable to the community. In a small community, the coordinator role may be part time. In a larger community, say of more than 500 members, the coordinator role should be full time. This is especially true if the community knowledge is of strategic value.

Critical mass

Communities of practice need a certain amount of interaction going on in order to remain in the consciousness of community members, and therefore to be a source of learning that people naturally turn to. They can suffer from being hidden, and communities that are too small or preoccupied to be sufficiently active will begin to lose their sense of identity, and people will forget they are there. Active online communities probably need at least one message a day on their message board or in their Q&A forum. The community coordinator therefore needs to build membership and grow the community as fast as possible after launch, to keep the momentum going, and get to critical mass as soon as possible. This will require a combination of marketing, advertising, awareness-raising and direct invitation to people who might be interested, which is likely to take a considerable portion of the community coordinator's time in the first few months after launch.

Each potential new member needs to be welcomed into the community, introduced to the terms of reference, and encouraged to take part in knowledge-sharing, thus building mass one member at a time. The size of the critical mass varies, depending on the intensity of the learning, the passion of the individuals, and how diverse they are culturally and geographically. For a colocated community of passionate experts working in a new field, the critical mass may be a dozen people. For a global community working in an established field, exchanging knowledge through email and online, the critical mass may be several hundred people.

A way to find each other

Communities must be visible. Staff must be able to find relevant communities, to join them easily, and to see who else is a community member. Ideally, the organisation should have some index or Yellow

Pages for the communities. In BP this function is provided by BP Connect, the Yellow Pages system, where each community has a page where it sets out its aims and objectives, lists the community members, and allows them to join or leave the community with one mouse click. In Conoco-Phillips, the communities are listed on the intranet, and each community has a home site where a click on the 'Join this community' button gains you community membership.

A community knowledge library

A community working on common processes and common topics needs its own knowledge library. This may be a community space within the corporate knowledge library as discussed in Chapter 10, and many large communities have their own portal. For example, Schlumberger spent $160 million to develop a knowledge base to store and share knowledge on technical solutions for the technical service community using the InTouchSupport.com system. Because customer support is Schlumberger's main business, the company felt that this investment was worthwhile. By cutting 95 per cent from the time it takes to answer a technical question, this technology has added a claimed annual value of $200 million, giving Schlumberger staff the ability to solve technical problems very rapidly, in a business where time is money.

Smaller communities may develop their own knowledge library, perhaps on a SharePoint site or as a community wiki. A community blog is often very useful to notify the community of any new lessons, new knowledge or updated processes in the library.

A social network

Communities of practice are one particular type of social network – one with the purpose of collective learning. The members of a community are happy to share lessons and knowledge with each other because they feel a sense of identity, and they are even happier to share their lessons with community members whom they know personally and feel a social connection with. Much work has been done in the field of knowledge management on buildings social networks, and the concept of social network analysis. This involves mapping out the social links and interactions within a community in order to assess the level of connectivity of the individuals. Certainly the community coordinator should be using any means possible to improve social connectivity, including using social software where appropriate. Social connectivity forms the groundwork for developing trust within the community, which is an essential ingredient if knowledge is to be shared and reused. However, assured and systematic learning within the community needs to transcend the social networks, and the community needs to develop processes and approaches for accessing the knowledge of people the individual members don't know and have never met. Approaches such as the Q&A forum, described above, allow knowledge sharing to take place within an entire community, linked by profession and business need, regardless of how socially connected the individuals may be.

A level of autonomy

In allowing communities of practice to exist and operate, the organisation is accepting that much of the knowledge lies with the practitioners, and that unwritten lessons can effectively be shared between them. The organisation must therefore give practitioners enough autonomy to act on the lessons they receive. They should be empowered to reuse lessons and process improvements that have been validated by the community, without necessarily getting their line manager to revalidate it every time. This does not mean that all decision-making is delegated to community members, but that line managers can delegate a certain level of technical assurance to communities. Disempowered communities rapidly become cynical and disaffected, which can become a bigger problem for management than having no communities at all.

A link with the explicit learning loop

Many valuable unwritten lessons can be exchanged in a community of practice. That doesn't mean that they have to stay unwritten. Once the lesson has been identified and shared, then the relevant process owner should take whatever action is needed either to write a new process, or to update the existing process. This implies that the process owners need to be very active in monitoring discussions within the community forum, and identifying new learning relevant to their particular process. In the Shell communities of practice, the subject matter experts (who are the Shell process owners) are required to monitor all discussions relevant to their particular process, and update the process documentation whenever they feel fit. This is part of their role description.

Peer assist

A peer assist is a meeting where the project team invites people with relevant knowledge and experience to come and share their lessons (written and unwritten) with the project team. Peer assists are one of the simplest and most effective ways of bringing the unwritten lessons into the team, and are so effective that many organisations, such as BP and De Beers, are making them mandatory for major projects. The success of peer assists depends on the following factors:

- *They need clear objectives*. The peers are bringing their lessons to the team for a purpose. The clearer you can be about that purpose, the more likely it is that the peer assist will deliver value. Sample objectives for a peer assist might be 'Develop a list of risks and issues' or 'Provide a list of options for cutting 50 per cent off the project budget'.
- *They should be focused on assisting*. Peer assists are meetings where the project team needs help and assistance, which is provided by the visiting peers. The project team members therefore need to be open to learning, and their peers need to be willing to share their lessons and experience. If the meeting falls into 'attack and defend' behaviours, then it has failed its purpose. This purpose will be most easily achieved if the peer assist is held early in the project, before the team has selected its preferred option, and if it is facilitated by someone external to the project.
- *They should truly involve peers of the project team*. These are not meetings where you bring in experts, technical authorities or senior managers. Bring in equivalent project managers and team members from previous projects who have personal experience and lessons to share. People are far more open to learning from, and sharing with, their peers, and this removes all the politics associated with management hierarchies.
- *They should have a four-part structure*. In the first part of the meeting, after the introductions and welcome, the project team explains what they know about the project context, the needs of the customer, the strategic objectives, and any local constraints they may be working under. In the second part of the meeting the peers discuss their knowledge and experience from previous projects. In the third part of the meeting the project team and the visiting peers go through a process of dialogue, often in small groups, as they attempt to use past experience to address the project team's issues. In the final part of the

meeting the visiting peers confer, then feed back their recommendations to the project team. A typical (and very powerful) example of a peer assist is shown in Case Study 11.1, from a company that was attempting to improve its marketing and distribution business in China.

> **Case Study 11.1 An attempt to improve marketing and distribution in China**
>
> Business results from China were poor, and it was proving difficult to generate the revenue that was expected. Staff held a peer assist in the Beijing office, and invited a range of managers from business units from other countries within the organisation to come and share the lessons from their marketing and distribution businesses. It became clear very quickly that some of the 'unwritten rules' of a successful business had not been transferred to China, and the peer assist quickly began to brainstorm a business plan, based on their own experience. The China team was not the only beneficiary of the meeting; at the end one of the managers from Mexico, who had attended as one of the peers, reported that he had taken notes during the peer assist discussions and now had written his own five-year business plan for Mexico.

Baton passing

Baton passing workshops were developed and used in Pfizer as a way for a project team to identify and transfer lessons from a project that has just finished, to one that is just starting a similar piece of work (although the baton passing meeting can be used solely by the project team as a method of lesson identification, similar to the retrospect described in Chapter 5). The workshop is usually a one-day or half-day meeting, held shortly after the end of the project while memories are still fresh. Good facilitation is essential.

The meeting starts with the project team reconstructing the process of the project, using Post-It notes to map all the key activities into a timeline along one of the walls of the meeting room. Key steps in the process are highlighted by the team. At the same time, the team members from the new project list the questions they would most like to have answered by the project team on different coloured Post-It notes below the timeline. Then the project team conducts a brainstorm to identify the learning points in the process. As discussed in Chapter 4, these tend to be the points where things did not go according to expectation, and either new challenges and pitfalls or new solutions and best practices are identified. These learning points are written by each participant on Post-It notes of a third colour, which are placed on the timeline as well. This process of brainstorming and charting acts to identify points in the process where the project team has lessons to share, and the future project team has questions to be answered.

For all of these points, discussions are held between the project team and the new project team to discuss and explore the lessons, until all the questions from the future project team have been answered. This discussion can usefully be recorded, and will form the raw material for documenting the lessons and putting them into the corporate lessons database.

The meeting finishes with a review of action planning. The future project team members review the actions they will take to incorporate the lessons, and those in the team from the completed project think about how they will take the actions forward into the rest of the company: how they will be validated, who will add them to the lessons database, who needs to be consulted, and who needs to take action.

Knowledge handover

Although a project may hold a series of after action reviews and retrospects to capture and document knowledge, it is also very good to supplement this by providing a forum where these lessons can be discussed, and where technical experts, process owners and project managers from other projects can ask further questions so they fully understand what has been learned and what the implications are. A knowledge handover provides such a forum.

A knowledge handover is a meeting at the end of a project, after the project team members have identified and captured their lessons learned, where they share and discuss these lessons with other projects and interested parties such as community leaders and subject matter experts. It is similar to a baton passing meeting, except that the learning points have already been identified, and the lessons have already been documented and added to the lessons database.

Sharing and seeking the unwritten lessons

One of the key points about the knowledge handover is that it should be driven by knowledge pull from the attendees, rather than by knowledge push from the project team. The attendees set the agenda. Before the event, the team circulates the list of lessons that they have captured (and may circulate the lessons themselves as well), and the attendees select which of the lessons they wish to discuss further in the handover meeting. These lessons are discussed in individual breakout sessions, and the attendees self-select which breakout sessions to attend.

It is good to kick off the formal part of the knowledge handover with an explanation of why it has been called, what its objectives and deliverables are, why it is important to the business, how it will be conducted, what the purpose of the recording is, and what the end product will be produced. Go through the agenda, discuss roles, and make sure everyone understands what they are there to do. It can be useful to start the knowledge handover with an introduction from the business sponsor (in person or by video) describing the importance of the exchange, and the business need. Then provide an overview of the project, its objectives, constraints and deliverables, so everyone can see the lessons in their context.

The individual lessons or groups of lessons are discussed in break-out sessions. This is where the majority of the lessons exchange happens. Divide the attendees into small groups of 8 to 20. Each group needs a facilitator and a scribe, who should be identified and briefed. The facilitator gets the dialogue going, but most of the time the conversation takes off rapidly and barely pauses for breath. The scribe needs to capture as much of the dialogue as possible, in the participants' words wherever possible, and note down who said what. (The session can also be recorded for later transcription, in case any additional lessons are identified.) About an hour may be needed, more if the groups are larger, for effective discussion.

The groups reconvene in the main room, and each group feeds back their findings for discussion in the wider group. The feedback sessions can usefully be recorded on audio or video. Also make sure you also record the details of the discussion that follows, as much valuable knowledge may be exchanged here as well.

The main outcome from the knowledge handover is an improved understanding of lessons which have already been recorded. The knowledge handover meeting is an opportunity for members of future projects to become clear about the actions they need to take, and for the process owners and technical authorities to be clear whether they need to update any process documentation.

Promoting conversation

Communities of practice, peer assists, baton passing and knowledge handover are all relatively formal ways of setting up conversations between people, to talk about lessons from the past, and how they may improve activity in the future. In addition to this, the company may want to consider how it can promote additional ad hoc conversation, but bear in mind that ad hoc conversations are not systems: if you are interested in systematic learning and performance improvement you need to be thinking about doing the rest of the activities described in this book as well. These are some approaches to promoting ad hoc conversation:

- *Move to an open plan office layout.* Closed doors and high walls stifle conversation. Although an open plan office does not guarantee that conversations will happen, it will remove some of the more concrete barriers.
- *Create communal areas where people can meet.* Put sofas and comfortable chairs next to the coffee machine. Put meeting tables together in an open area. Create spaces that allow for chance encounters. GCHQ in the UK (the government communications headquarters, which is the centre for Her Majesty's Government Signal Intelligence) designed its entire building with the intent of creating the possibility of chance meetings, placing the offices in two concentric rings with a wide corridor between the two. This is the 'main street', which everybody needs to walk along; it contains break-out areas, chairs and tables where people can hold impromptu meetings.
- *Set up an online Yellow Pages system,* so that people can easily find the contact details of others who have relevant knowledge and experience. Make it easy for people to find experts and practitioners who will be able to share lessons with them.
- *Promote online conversation.* Introduce social software such as discussion forums, management blogs or social networking sites. Allow open discussion, but not anonymous discussion, on any and all topics.
- *Hold town hall meetings, round table meetings, briefings and Q&A sessions with managers.* Make sure the managers listen as well as talk.

12

The governance of lesson learning

You can have the best technology, all the roles in place, processes defined as part of your work process, but that doesn't mean lessons will be learned. You can have the best system in the world for lesson learning, it won't necessarily be used. You need actually to embed the habits of learning and applying lessons into the culture and working practices of the organisation in such a way that it is sustained. Remember that the second biggest barrier quoted in the survey described in Chapter 1 was the lack of support from senior management. This lack of support results in lack of motivation, prioritisation and governance, even if there is no lack of process, technology or roles.

The introduction of any new management system into an organisation requires a change in culture. For example, when you introduce customer relationship management you have to change the way you react with clients. When companies introduced people management, they had to change the culture of interaction between management and employees. When financial management was introduced centuries ago, there was a culture change in the rigour with which money was handled and accounted for. If any change to a new management system is to deliver value in the long term, then there needs to be a way of changing the culture, and of making sure that the behaviours stay changed, the processes are carried out, and the people do what they are supposed to do.

As far as financial management is concerned, there is a clearly defined compliance standard that defines what acceptable financial management is, and any company that wants to operate in the marketplace abides by the standard, and plays by the rules. If the rules are broken, there are sanctions and punishments, as the directors of Enron found out to their cost. These rules, standards and sanctions are partly responsible for ensuring that good financial management is widespread and sustained, despite the odd bad apple.

As yet, there are few if any standards, rules and sanctions for lesson learning. If lesson learning is to be sustained, it will be sustained by factors internal to individual organisations, as well as by the enthusiasm and belief of practitioners. However, this enthusiasm is not endless, and the introduction of a lesson learning system often falls into a familiar pattern:

- an announcement that 'we are going to become a learning organisation'
- the introduction of new processes, accountabilities and technologies
- some early wins, some high profile successes
- after a while, people get too busy to bother, as they find that learning is not a high priority for senior managers, and that there is no comeback if they don't apply the processes, use the technologies or deliver against their accountabilities
- gradual dwindling away of lesson learning.

Why does this happen? What is missing? Is there something that we can learn from the implementation of other successfully sustained management practices? I think there is – the concept of a governance framework for lesson learning that defines and sustains the priority set by senior management.

A governance framework

If you are a manager and you want to get something done in your organisation, you need to do three things:

- make it very clear what you want done
- give people the tools and the training to do it
- check that they have done what you want.

This is true in all areas of life. If you wanted to get your teenage son or daughter to mow the lawn, for example, you would first be very clear with them what you expected them to do; you would show them where the lawnmower is, and teach them how to use it; then you would check that they really have done it. Without the clarity of expectation and explanation, they would most likely claim that they weren't sure what to do and so not do it, or else they would half-do the job, leaving the edges untrimmed and the grass clippings all over the lawn. If you don't give them the lawnmower and show them how to use it, they wouldn't be able to get started anyway, and if you didn't check up on them, the likelihood is that they might be distracted by more urgent activities such as the PlayStation, or instant messaging their friends.

The governance of lesson learning

Again if we look at financial management, everybody in the organisation is clear about what is expected of them. They know that they will have to prepare budgets at the start of any significant piece of work, have to do cost tracking as the work continues, and have to balance the books at the end of the job. They will have the tools to do these activities, such as SAP or Excel spreadsheets, and they will have the training they need. They also know that management will be checking that they have done what they are supposed to do, and there may well be periodic audits to check compliance against expectations. Whether or not the employees believe that financial management is a good thing, the company has put in place a framework to ensure that it happens.

Those three elements – clarity of expectation, the tools to do the job, and monitoring – make sure the job gets done and gets done in the manner in which you want it done. They form a governance framework for mowing the lawn, or for financial management. The same three elements are needed in a governance framework for organisational learning, as described below and shown in Figure 12.1. There must be:

- a set of clear corporate expectations for how lessons will be identified and reapplied within the organisation, and the definition of a set of learning processes that are expected of all staff
- the means to operate a complete lesson learning loop, which will include:
  - roles and accountabilities for lesson identification, process ownership and lessons review
  - processes for identifying, validating and reviewing lessons
  - technologies for storing, sorting, tracking, finding and publishing lessons
- a person or team monitoring and measuring the application of the lesson learning system to:
  - make sure that people are delivering on their accountabilities, and applying the system in the way that they are expected to
  - identify the need for new interventions to improve the system, and ensure there is continuous improvement in the ability of the organisation to learn from experience
  - report to senior management on the application of the learning system and people's delivery against the expectations.

Figure 12.1 Governance framework

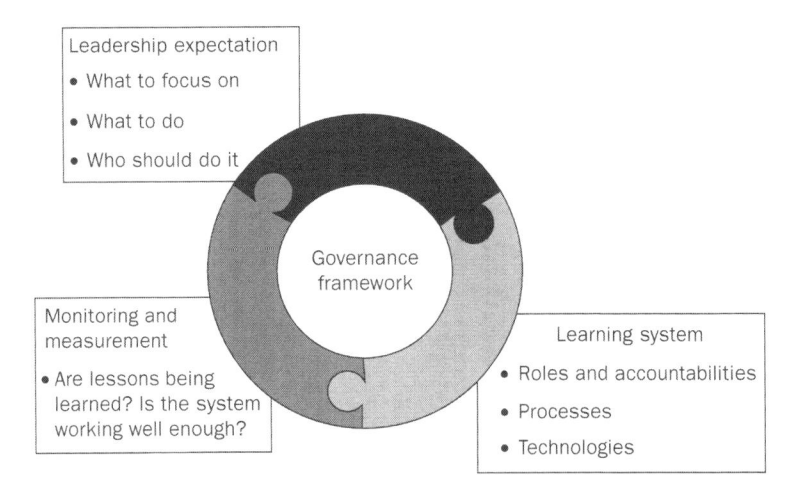

Leadership expectation
- What to focus on
- What to do
- Who should do it

Governance framework

Monitoring and measurement
- Are lessons being learned? Is the system working well enough?

Learning system
- Roles and accountabilities
- Processes
- Technologies

These three elements are shown in Figure 12.1 as the interlocked pieces of a jigsaw, because if any one of them is missing, the lesson learning system won't operate:

- If the corporate expectations are missing, nobody knows what they are supposed to be doing about lesson learning.
- If the roles and accountabilities are missing, nobody knows whether it is their job or not.
- If the processes are missing, nobody knows how they should be identifying or reusing lessons.
- If the technologies are missing, nobody has the ability to store, search, find or track lessons.
- If the monitoring and measuring is missing, managers are not aware whether the system is being applied or working; then people can get away without using the system, and therefore don't bother.

Let us look at the three elements in more detail.

Make corporate expectations clear

Senior managers in the organisation need to make clear their expectations for lesson learning by explicitly stating what needs to be done, and by whom. They need to write these expectations down, and keep reinforcing them by what they say. They also need to make sure these expectations do not get weakened by, or conflict with, other company structures and expectations.

One clear way to define expectations is to define an *in-house standard* for lesson learning. What does lesson learning mean in practice? What is an acceptable level of lesson learning activity? Does every project need to hold a retrospect, or only the big ones? When, during the project lifecycle, should lesson identification meetings be held? Are after action reviews expected, and if so, then when? Are peer assists a mandatory requirement, or optional? You need to sit down with senior managers and decide what the internal corporate lesson learning standard is going to be. For example, in one engineering company, each project is required:

- to develop a knowledge management plan to review lessons from previous projects
- to assign a knowledge manager to manage this plan
- to hold a lessons identification review at the end of the major project stages.

These expectations are written out clearly, and have been rolled out to all project staff.

The lesson learning standard needs to be set at the right level. It needs to be just sufficient to deliver value, without loading too much onerous process onto the business. The standard may need to set different levels of lesson learning activity depending on the scale of business activity. You may require lower levels of lesson learning activity for projects costing less than $1 million than you would for projects costing over $10 million. Production or service areas of your organisation might need different lesson learning activities from project areas. The key, however, is to be clear about what the organisation expects in terms of lesson learning activity for each area of the business.

Along with clarity on standards comes clarity on *accountability*: whose job is it to ensure the lesson learning activity takes place? Whose job is it to make sure the actions are assigned? Who are the process owners? Senior managers need to set up one or more chains of accountability, so everyone in the organisation knows what is expected of them. We say 'one or more' chains – in many organisations there will be three chains of accountability, as shown in Figure 12.2.

There will certainly be a chain of accountability in the line organisation – the organisation of business units that 'do the work'. Here the accountability will be about compliance to the lesson learning standard for operational work, including identifying lessons from completed work and reusing lessons in future work. For example, the Head of the European Division may

The Lessons Learned Handbook

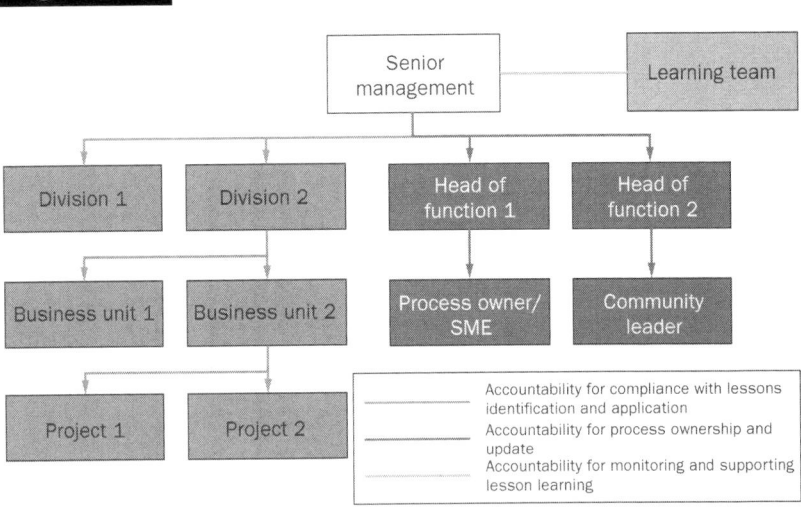

Figure 12.2 Chains of accountability in an organisation

```
                    Senior
                  management ─────────── Learning team
        ┌────────────┬──────────┬──────────┐
    Division 1   Division 2   Head of     Head of
                              function 1  function 2
        │            │            │            │
    Business     Business    Process owner/  Community
    unit 1       unit 2         SME           leader
        │            │
    Project 1    Project 2
```

———— Accountability for compliance with lessons identification and application
———— Accountability for process ownership and update
———— Accountability for monitoring and supporting lesson learning

be accountable for lesson learning in Europe, and will devolve this to the country managers, who will in turn pass this responsibility to unit managers. The unit managers will then check that the individual projects or production lines are doing what they should be doing to identify and apply lessons.

In a matrix organisation there may also be a chain of accountability in the functional or support departments. Here the accountability is likely to cover the ownership, maintenance and deployment of the company knowledge base, and will include accountabilities for process ownership and community leadership. The head of marketing, for example, will be accountable for making sure that the company's marketing processes are managed and updated, and will ensure that the individual process owners and community leaders are doing their job properly.

Finally, there will be a set of accountabilities for the lesson learning support team. These will include accountability for maintaining the lesson learning system, and monitoring and measuring its use.

Senior managers can be clear about what they expect of lesson learning by publishing standards and setting clear accountabilities. They also need to make sure that their expectations are supported by what they say and do. For example, they must assign the time and resource needed to manage knowledge, and make sure that the reward and recognition system in the organisation is supportive of lesson learning. There is no point, for example, in expecting high levels of collaboration from business units, and at the same time rewarding internal competition by sponsoring 'factory of the year awards' (see Case Study 1.2).

Lesson learning systems

At the same time as making their expectations for lesson learning very clear, senior managers must make sure that staff in the organisation are fully equipped to deliver against these expectations. They need a lesson learning system. They need a lessons database. They need training in lesson identification processes. They need community of practice technology, a good search engine, and wikis, blogs and portals. They need facilitation for peer assists, retrospects, baton passing meetings and after action reviews. The complexity of this lesson learning system will vary considerably. Small organisations, colocated in a single office, may be able to use very simple tools and processes to manage their knowledge. When I operated a local lesson learning system in BP Norway in the mid-1990s, it was supported by simple end-of-project after action reviews and a paper file of identified lessons. A large multinational company, on the other hand, with hundreds of thousands of employees spread around the globe, will need more sophisticated systems, with custom-built technology and well-defined processes.

Monitoring and measurement

Monitoring and measurement are key to the long-term sustainability of lesson learning and the lesson learning culture. What gets measured gets done. What doesn't get measured gets pushed to the side by other 'more important' work. Measurement, linked to reward and recognition, shows that the company is serious about lesson learning. There would be no point in setting standards, if there were no measurement against those standards.

Metrics

There are three main areas where you might consider measuring: compliance, activity and output:

- *Compliance measurement* involves measuring degrees of compliance with the lesson learning standard. How many parts of the business are up to standard? How many projects are holding retrospects or baton passing meetings? How many process owners have well-documented processes?
- *Activity measurement* looks at the lesson learning activity that is taking place. How many lessons are being entered into the lessons

databases? How many questions are being asked and answered on the community forums? How frequently are the company best practices being updated? What percentage of lessons is being closed out?

- *Output measurement* looks at the results of the lesson learning activity. Are costs decreasing? Are projects being completed to budget and on time? Is the bidding process more successful?

One business that I have worked with tracks the activity measures closely and each quarter measures and reports for each unit of the business:

- the number of new lessons identified
- the number of lessons closed
- the number of process documents updated
- the number of new process documents created
- the estimated total value of the lessons.

In addition, they track and report their main metric, which is the cost per unit production. Although more factors than learning affect this metric, improved learning should still be correlated with improved performance.

In an online presentation Brookhaven Science Laboratories lists the following metrics:

- the number of internal lessons learned submissions and distributions
- the number of external lessons learned submissions and distributions
- lessons learned sources reviewed
- most viewed lessons
- timeliness of distribution of internal and external lessons learned
- user data (unique user, user searches, user organisation)
- feedback (applicability, corrective actions, procedure revision, training revisions, and so on)
- data stream trending for lessons learned
- work control (pre- and post-job lessons learned)
- lessons learned origin (occurrences, operating experience, assessments, critiques, and so on) (BNL, 2008).

A third example of metrics comes from Ford, which was a pioneer in formal lesson push systems. Their best practice replication system was highly metricated, as shown in Case Study 12.1.

Case Study 12.1 The Ford best practice replication system

The Ford best practice replication system operated across 37 manufacturing plants in Ford, and covered 25 process areas, each one associated with a community of practice. One 'focal point' was assigned per community per plant, accountable for managing the system locally, and a central support team provided governance for the system as a whole.

Process improvements were identified at the plants through a number of mechanisms, such as quality circles, problem solving and incident analysis. Each week, the focal point would put any new best practices into the best practice replication database, housed on the web, using purpose built software. The best practice would describe the process improvement, with diagrams if needed, and with contact details of the originating team. The software would then automatically forward the best practice to the other focal points.

As a result, each focal point would receive five to eight best practices each week, and they were required to decide for each of them how the improved process would be implemented in their plant. Then they would report back, through the system, whether they:

- would apply the improvement
- would reject the improvement (giving reasons why it did not apply to them, such as not applicable or not economically feasible)
- had already applied the improvement
- were still investigating.

If they had applied the improvement, they had to report how much it had saved them.

These replies were compiled and reported on a scorecard to management at quarterly meetings.

The result for Ford was excellent. During the period 1996–2000 the company added $855 million in value to its operations, with over 2,600 best practices replicated in the assembly plants. In fact, 40 per cent of the plant task was eventually being made through replication.

Reward and sanction

Together with monitoring and measurement comes reward and sanction. Parts of the business that perform well in lesson learning should be rewarded or recognised, and parts that choose to ignore their lesson learning accountabilities should face some form of sanction. If there is no sanction against opting out of the lesson learning system, then the organisation is effectively sending the message that lesson learning is optional. In an increasingly busy world, optional activity does not get done.

Any company that is serious about lesson learning needs to be serious about sanctions. The metrics need to be transparent, reported at a high level, and linked to rewards and sanctions. For example, in the UK Army, metrics for lesson learning (including the percentage of lesson-related actions which have actually been completed) are reported at an annual meeting chaired by the vice chief of defence staff – one of the most senior UK defence officials. Few individuals want their failure to complete their assigned actions to be reported at so high a level. As a result, actions tend to get done!

Avoid inconsequential rewards or those that promote the wrong behaviour. One company rewarded people only on the number of lessons they submitted to the lessons database. Every year, immediately before the metrics were recorded, there was a flood of poor quality, low value, badly written lessons. This just devalued the whole process.

The supporting organisation

Maintaining and coordinating the lesson learning system, including conducting measurement and metrics, needs to be the responsibility of an individual and team. Their main tasks will be keeping the system maintained (updating technology, training people in the processes, coaching individuals with lesson learning roles), running the monitoring, measurement and reporting, crafting the longer term learning strategy, and making any interventions needed to sustain lesson learning. In the US Army, this is the role of the Centre for Army lessons learned. In another defence contractor, learning coordinators are assigned within the business units to measure and support lesson learning. However the supporting organisation is set up, there needs to be someone coordinating and monitoring lessons learned. Without this support, lesson learning cannot be sustained.

Reference

Brookhaven National Laboratory (2008) BNL Lessons Learned Workshop, presented by E. Sierra, 27 June, *http://www.bnl.gov/qmo/linkable_files/ppt/ LL%20Talk%206-27-08.ppt* (accessed 6 February 2010).

13

The principles and processes of safety investigations

Johnny Martin

Johnny Martin is highly experienced in the techniques of safety-related learning. In his many years working for BP he was involved in many incident investigations, from minor occurrences to serious events, which included fatality. He was coordinator of the Operations Excellence community, owner of the Operations Excellence portal, and one of the instigators and coordinator of the Operations Value Process (a company-wide self-audit process, with a strong emphasis on performance and process safety).

Safety is one of the prime metrics by which our modern businesses and companies measure themselves. In some cases external bodies have measured that metric and found that the targets haven't been hit. Historically the first reaction was to improve personal safety, then the safe environment was added, and now there is the addition of the sometimes forgotten area of operational and equipment safety, with a great emphasis on the concept of process safety.

Safety is an area where we can all learn lessons from each other freely. The underlying causes or factors of most incidents are the same across industry, and are probably found in a combination of organisational, technical, systemic and/or human failures. However, this learning has not proved easy, and failures in investigation, root cause analysis, reporting, lessons storage or retrieval commonly make it hard to recycle these common factors into new learnings, new actions and change. Yet some industries have found the key to effective lesson learning in safety, and work this all in a very detailed way.

What happened and why?

Let us explore this paragraph:

> It is tested in 1,100 degrees C for an hour, it has to survive 200 degrees C continuously for 10 hours, withstand 3,400g, not crush at 20,000 feet in the ocean, and be large enough to be found without being too heavy for its host.

The black box recorder (flight data recorder to give it its proper name) has had a major impact on aircraft safety since its creation in the 1930s and its modern development from the mid-1950s. It was required because the aircraft industry needed to understand 'what happened and why' so it could set about learning what went wrong, and make changes for the better. These key lessons could be fed into engineering modifications, systemic changes, pilot training in flight simulators and so on.

Why? Because the aircraft industry is a high reliability organisation, where the consequences of failure are unacceptable. Other examples of high reliability organisations are air traffic control, the nuclear industry and neurosurgery.

Can we learn from how high reliability organisations approach safety learning? To do this, we have to go back to the basics of why things go wrong, how incidents are investigated and reported, and how change happens as a result. In other words, we need to look at where the learning data comes from, and where it goes.

Imagine that something has gone wrong at your company, in one of your businesses or in your industry. The lessons that came from that event investigation might be very clear, pointing to errors or faults. You look at these lessons and realise that you have the same or similar errors or faults elsewhere in your systems. You find them and are able to fix them through engineering modification or by changing your management processes.

This is of course a very simple learning cycle, and in essence the same as the one described in Chapter 2. Although situations are more complex, the principles of this cycle apply to any investigation. The skill of the investigator and depth and quality of their investigation will determine the quality of the recommendations and lessons, and deliver a learning organisation that builds on the principles of continuous improvement; one that understands its gaps, closes them in timely fashion and looks for the next set of gaps. Such an investigator constantly asks 'what if?', and if the 'what if?' were to happen then 'what is the worst that could result?' They chase that down, covering all possibilities. The workforce is highly motivated and empowered to stop work where they feel it is unsafe, and defects are picked up very early, like long wave vibrations! Now you are acting like a high reliability organisation and are focusing on failure as well as success.

However, as we know, things will go wrong, and if the worst does happen then you need to understand what happened and why. You have to get to the level of data that the black box can give you, so you need people skilled in root cause failure analysis, who can track down the answers to 'why?' in an investigation, and draw out quality recommendations and real lessons which can be embedded into a change programme. As we go through the rest of this chapter we will look at the practicalities of investigation, simple root cause analysis techniques and the reporting processes that can then populate a lessons learned system.

The investigation process

To be effective in the skill of investigating safety procedures, you need to be prepared, and have clear objectives, trained people and a close out process that captures the corrective actions or lessons. This investigation process can be split into three elements:

- preparation
- reporting the incident and first steps
- formal analysis (including identifying corrective actions and lesson identification).

Let us look at these elements individually.

Preparation

You should have in place a full suite of emergency procedures that cover everything from emergency response to incident investigation, including interview guidance. This will support the training and development of skilled accident and incident investigators and will be underpinned by a rigorous set of objectives, which describe why you are carrying out the investigation, and what the expected outcomes are.

As part of the emergency response procedure there needs to be a list of the people who require to be called, which should be a live document that reflects the current leadership structure. So much time is lost when personnel don't know who to call and when.

It is best practice to compile an investigator's toolkit, which might include:

- an evidence logbook
- a lessons learned worksheet
- pens, ink and a marker
- pencils, rulers and erasers
- a clipboard with plain paper and graph paper
- tags for evidence
- flipcharts, butchers' paper, or a roll of newsprint paper and yellow stickies for a timeline
- a digital camera and possibly a video camera
- a voice recorder
- high visibility tape
- sellotape
- measuring tapes (0–5m and 0–30m wide)
- a compass
- a magnifying glass
- plastic bags
- a first-aid kit
- a high visibility bag to contain all these materials.

It is important that investigators have the proper tools prepared well before they need them, as this speeds up their ability to respond and ensures the early capture of evidence, which might otherwise be lost in the early stages.

Reporting the incident and first steps

Reporting and subsequent steps should be based on the potential severity, degree of injury or extent of damage during the incident. If the personnel have well-developed and well-practised procedures and emergency responses (also known as gun drills – when the military strip down their weapons, clean and rebuild them; usually seen and marvelled at by the public at military displays and the result of practice, practice, practice), a very quick and clear assessment can be made and reported.

The initial reporter or investigator of the event must quickly establish that there is no possibility of an escalation or secondary incident. For example, if someone collapses, it has to be established whether they have done so as a result of a toxic or inert atmosphere. There is no point in people rushing to the rescue and falling foul of the same hazard. So it is important to be aware of the potential hazards in the workplace and to be intimate with the incident plan and emergency response procedures.

It is worth having a brief checklist to assess the scene for additional or secondary dangers or hazards, which might include the following questions:

- Have the personnel moved away from the scene?
- Is the equipment shutdown?
- Have the power sources been turned off?
- Has the leak, spill or dangerous material been confined?
- Is the workplace ventilated?
- Has someone administered first aid? (First aid might not be possible until some or all of the above has occurred.)
- Has someone carried out an initial clean-up? (Sometimes it might be important that there is no clean-up if it is important to preserve evidence. Some investigators prefer that a clean-up is carried out under their presence.)

Securing the scene and preserving the evidence is critical to any investigation, whether it is simple or highly complex. This may fall to the personnel on the ground before the investigator or investigation team arrives, and shouldn't be delayed, so clear and practised procedures will be invaluable at this stage.

The initial investigator has to try to form a rough understanding of what happened, and this can be established by asking:

- Who is injured (how many)?
- What happened?
- Who saw it or heard it?
- What were the steps leading to the incident?
- What is the extent of equipment or property damage?
- What actions contributed to the incident?
- When did the actions or steps occur?
- Where did each action or step occur?
- How or why did the contact occur?

These questions would form the basis of a good starting point for the investigation, and should be debriefed to the investigation team on their arrival.

Formal analysis

Generally the more severe the injuries or damage in an incident, the greater the need to collect, record and preserve the evidence in order to understand what caused it. This is the core part of the investigation and therefore involves the largest workload. Collecting evidence can include collecting instrument or computer data, consulting documents and permits, and identifying witnesses. This can be done by considering the people, equipment, positioning and data involved.

When the investigation team arrives they should carry out preliminary data review, part of which will be the debrief supplied by the initial investigator. They should then start to collect parts, tools or materials that document any of the circumstances of the incident. In some cases, a thorough examination of machines, tools and so on by an expert may be required to establish failure modes in a precise way.

Create some record of the relevant locations of people, parts and materials. Photography and or video are often used in important cases, especially if the scene cannot be preserved. If this equipment is not available then a simple sketch will serve the purpose. Be sure to indicate the relationship of objects to each other, and where the witnesses were located. This can be done with indicators, arrows or highlights to show important or relevant items or objects.

What documents should be gathered? Look for standards, written instructions, procedures, task analysis, risk assessments, job hazard analysis logs (hand written or computer based), charts, material labels, equipment identification markings, maintenance records and transport movement logs. This list is not exhaustive, but it shows the range of evidence that might be available to you to help deliver a thorough investigation.

As you will have seen many times in police dramas or reality investigations, once evidence is disturbed or changed it is sometimes impossible to recreate the scene and therefore understand what happened. Never forget that well-intentioned people sometimes act out of character to try to skew the investigation away from blame. These people are under enormous pressure and for reasons they cannot explain later they may try to make the situation 'better' in their eyes. There is a key point here and it is covered elsewhere in this chapter. The reason for the investigation is to determine what happened and why, not to apportion blame.

A useful technique is to try to visualise the incident. The more investigations you are involved in, the more you acquire this skill, hence the gun drill analogy. You do this mentally or, if the situation allows, physically walk through the incident. Sometimes clues can be gained by taking up the position of the injured party in the case of a workface incident. Another option is to talk through the high level events with people closest to or knowledgeable in the area.

On a site visit look for physical conditions that may have contributed to the incident: height, depth, width, light, atmosphere, noise and temperature. Use your senses. What do you see, hear and smell, and how does it all 'feel' to you?

Investigating people

The next aspect of your investigation is to determine who witnessed what. The names of witnesses should come from the initial investigator or the first person on the scene. There are two types of witness, an eye or direct witness and indirect witness. It is important to separate those who saw or heard, and those who have indirect or secondary information. At this stage you are looking for facts, so look for people who have valid knowledge or information that can help establish what happened.

Interviewing is an art form in itself (see chapters 3 and 4) and you have to ensure that you or your investigators are fully trained and have excellent people skills. They have to be able to establish rapport, as a poor interview technique can be very disruptive and become a barrier to establishing the root causes of the event. There are many organisations and materials that teach interviewing techniques, and we give a basic summary here. Remember that if an incident is severe then the whole investigation will be taken out of your hands altogether by the authorities or regulator.

Interviewing

If a witness or witnesses has observed a severe incident then they may be traumatised, so it is essential to ensure that they are mentally and physically in good enough shape to be involved in the interview process. Witnesses have to be selected for their ability to contribute to the investigation. If there is more than one witness, interview the one who knows most about the incident first. The more they know, the quicker they should be interviewed.

It helps if you can carry out interviews in a private, comfortable and neutral location. Make clear to the witness at the outset how you will record the interview, and establish their agreement. Recording can be via audio, video or handwritten notes, and in severe cases by using a court style recorder. If audio or video is used, transcribe the text as soon as practical after the interview.

Try to have a standard set of questions available to you, which will allow you to follow a line of questioning. This will keep you on track, provide consistency and ensure you don't miss anything.

Keep as much of the evidence that you gathered with you as possible as you may have to use it to review with the witness, but only do this once you have heard their account. This is essential as you don't want to influence the witness or lead them down a wrong path.

When interviewing watch out for and explore further if necessary:

- an act or acts committed incorrectly
- errors of omission
- a sequence error, when someone does something in the process out of sequence
- details of timing, when an act is not performed at the allotted time.

These points represent the branches in the questioning tree described in Chapter 4.

As you go through your investigation you will sometimes come up against non-fact or supposition. These are second-hand testimonies or hearsay from witnesses or others. Suppositions could be made up from conclusions reached by witnesses or other people. Supposition may eventually turn out to be factual or part fact after careful investigation, but you must record it as non-fact or supposition until it is proven fact. Later when we talk about timeline construction you must mark any supposition as just that.

The interview process

These are the stages of an interview:

- *Establishing rapport.* If you don't know the witness, begin with an introduction, explain who you are and (where appropriate) give a very brief insight about your experience. Allow the witness the same opportunity. Explain the investigation process, the objectives (to prevent reoccurrence) and the interviewee's role in helping that process. Make it clear that the process is not to apportion blame, but to find out what happened and why. Check that the interviewee understands this and use non-threatening language.
- *Narrative.* You are trying to establish an account of what the person saw or heard. They may be like a coiled spring, so it is important to let them tell their story uninterrupted. Make notes, but don't ask any questions until the witness has finished their account. If questions occur to you make a note of them to ask later. Experience demonstrates that this is the best method to gain a quality insight into what

happened and why. Some people may go off at a tangent; your job is to keep them on track. However, try to note what the tangent was and come back to it later; it may have relevance to the investigation.

- *Interaction.* Once the witness has finished their narrative, it may be time to take a comfort break. Have one in any case. This will give you the opportunity to take stock of what you heard and let you think about how you will open the next phase, which will be your questions for clarification. As you go through this part of the interview, avoid asking leading questions and use the verification or reflection technique of repeating back to the witness what you just heard. If possible use the language of the witness, repeat and use terms they used. Use the documented evidence that you have gathered as an aid to gain more insight and information. Explore other previous incidents with similar causes in the area.

- *Conclusion.* Now you come full circle with the witness. Summarise their account to confirm you have recorded the facts accurately. It is best practice at this stage to ask, 'Is there anything else you would like to add, regardless of how unimportant it may seem to you?' Then pause for what will feel like an uncomfortable period. This is a reflective time that allows the witness to search for any insignificant piece of information. Finally, thank the witness for their contribution and mention any follow-up items that may require a review for clarification. Remind them of the next steps in the process and targets for reporting back. Given them your contact details and encourage them to get in touch with you if they remember any other information, no matter how insignificant it may seem to them.

Investigating equipment

Equipment includes any part that has failed or is thought to have contributed to the cause of the incident. You or your investigators may require further expert analysis of this physical evidence. However, valuable information can often be obtained by examining the equipment as soon as possible before it is removed for further analysis.

It is extremely important to inspect the personal protective equipment, tools, parts and equipment involved in the incident. Computers and computer controlled systems should be diagnostically checked for hardware or software failures. Samples of raw materials, process fluids, solids or any chemicals that may have formed due to a reaction in the incident can be analysed. If samples before the incident are available analyse them as well.

Investigating positioning

Positioning is recorded by your photos, sketches or diagrams, and refers to the locations of people and equipment before and after the incident. The final resting place of people and equipment is a key part of the evidence, which helps investigators to understand the scale of the event.

It is important to check and note the condition of personal protective equipment or tools used or found at the scene. This is a useful quick checklist of questions to consider, which will help you collect physical evidence:

- Which side of the equipment is affected?
- What is the top, what is the bottom?
- What was underneath what?
- How far was a person or equipment moved?
- What is blown and what is not?
- Were there skid marks and if so from where to where?
- Is there evidence of oily or wet surfaces?

You should now begin to see how important the different forms of evidence are, and how important it is to preserve the scene of the event so that sketches, photographs or video can capture the overall scene. Gathering as much information as possible about the positioning of people, equipment, materials and the surrounding environment is very important.

Investigating data

Data comes in many forms across the workplace, and can be a simple as a written log or order, or as complex as a computer-based work management system. Irrespective of whether the data evidence is hand written or electronic, it has to be gathered. It can be helpful to split the data into two groups:

- information records – such as company standards, policies and procedures; these can form a substantial list
- physical environment records – such as site layout, building plans and traffic flow. Although these records can result in a shorter list it is nevertheless very important.

Organising the evidence

Once you have gathered all your evidence, you must organise it. You should have your logbook up to date, with all the evidence logged in it and each piece of evidence assigned a number.

As you start to collect evidence, you may in the very early stages start to identify the root causes behind the accident incidents, and recognise corrective actions and lessons learned (the processes of recognising actions and arising lessons are described in more detail below). Start to make a note of these lessons on a lessons learned worksheet.

Review the consolidated worksheet with investigation team members, experts (local, federal or external) and other participants, to gain consensus, and to verify and validate the lessons to be communicated. Also speak to the leaders of the organisation, to understand the organisational impact of gathering evidence and agree a method of dissemination.

Check your witness list to make sure that you have completed all initial and follow-up interviews. Identify and label all the sketches, photographs and video tapes or cards.

Ensure that analysis results have all been returned to you, that nothing is missed, and that you have expert testing results to hand.

Now it is time to process all the evidence that has been gathered. The next series of steps is to build a timeline with all the critical factors mapped onto it. This can be started at the outset of your investigation, so you can populate as you go. Ensure you cover all processes used in the investigation and add any additional lessons learned to the worksheet. Remember that not all lessons are low points or failings; there may be successes to share such as the initial handling of the incident. Be alert to all types of lessons.

Identify the critical factors. These are the negative undesirable conditions or causes that influenced the course of events. To explain this further – if these critical factors could have been eliminated or didn't exist, then the occurrence would have been prevented or the severity reduced. So critical factors point us to the areas that need to be examined further.

The severity of the incident will dictate the size of the material you will require to draw the timeline on. In BP we found that having a smallish roll of newsprint paper was ideal for this, as we only tore off what we required.

The timeline may cover 1–2 hours divided up in 15-minute segments, or it may cover days, weeks or even months. Longer timelines will be needed if you have discovered that there were previous or similar incidents that need to be captured, together with their contributing critical factors.

Start by capturing the general sequence of events and conditions, so that the investigation team can see the incident unfold in chronological order. Use sticky labels to map the data onto the time line, as these can be easily moved around as more information is known. You can also use pencils initially to draw lines between the building blocks or sticky labels, as pencil lines can be easily erased or changed.

Observe gaps in the timeline and investigate these gaps, resolve contradictions in evidence and re-interview witnesses if necessary.

The benefits of timelines are that they:

- are invaluable in the organisation of your evidence
- are a good guide for the investigation
- help to validate a sequence of events
- identify critical factors and their relationships
- assist with the root cause analysis
- simplify the organisation and preparation of the close out report.

The final analysis

The evidence has now been gathered and the timeline drawn. Now it is time to analyse this body of work. The key to effective analysis is to identify the root causes, and develop the corrective actions and lessons to be communicated.

There are quite a few techniques used for analysing the basic root causes. One of the most widely accepted is the loss causation model of Den Norske Veritas – Systematic Cause Analysis Technique (SCAT), which portrays the factors creating or causing loss-producing events. It is a practical, easy-to-remember way of seeing and understanding the circumstances which can result in loss.

Another popular method is 'the five whys' technique, which is a very simple but powerful process for identifying the causes of an incident. It brain storms 'why' the incident happened and/or 'why' the unfavourable conditions existed. It can be used by an individual working on their own or with a group of people.

This is the methodology for using the five whys technique:

- Select an event associated with the incident.
- Ask why this event occurred.
- Solicit as many sub-events or conditions as possible.
- For each sub-event or condition, ask why it occurred.

- Record these sub-events or conditions on a tree type chart.
- Repeat the process up to five times, each time digging down to a deeper level of 'why'.

The process need not require all five iterations to get to the root or system cause(s). When you get to a level that shows that some management function is out of control, or when going any further doesn't really add any value to the investigation, then that branch of the tree should be considered complete.

The advantage of this technique is that it is a very simple and straightforward process. Effective use of a flipchart along with your timeline will allow a group to keep track of responses and select the important roots to pursue. Minimal training is necessary, although judgement, experience and a positive attitude are very important team member attributes and contribute substantially to the successful discovery of the incident's root or system cause(s).

The disadvantage is that the technique might not be appropriate for use in the investigation of very complex incidents, where a more formal root cause failure analysis such as SCAT should be used. Also it relies on having people available with appropriate knowledge and experience on the system being investigated.

No matter what system or technique you use, remember:

- not to jump to conclusions
- that causes must be supported by evidence
- that your analysis should describe the incident, thoroughly, accurately and completely.

Identifying corrective actions and lesson identification

Once the root causes have been identified, it is time to draw out the corrective actions and the lessons. This is the point where everything you gathered in, drew and wrote is brought to a conclusion and corrective action proposals are developed. These will all be recorded in your final report, and will result in the lessons from the incident being truly learned, either in your business unit, across the businesses or across the industry.

The root cause analysis is where the true value of the investigation is found and it is the quality of this part of the investigation that will uncover the correct causes, and allow you to develop corrective actions, which come out of the root cause. Once you have identified that cause, then you or the team or the expert will have to decide on the corrective action required to fix the problem to prevent reoccurrence or reduce the risk. Corrective actions may include:

- introducing new processes
- replacing equipment
- redesigning equipment
- repositioning equipment
- rewriting job descriptions
- reorganising management processes.

So the corrective action can be simple and easy, or it can be very difficult. If the corrective action is significant enough, then the business may not be able to make any corrections, and this would mean getting out of the business. If the corrective actions are too broad it is likely that the true cause is not understood and therefore identifying the lessons to apply will make no sense.

To help you to decide how to communicate the lessons, be aware that if the cause of the incident is procedural in nature then the solution should be procedural; if the cause is engineering then the solution should involve engineering. Ensure that each cause identified in the report is linked to one of the corrective actions.

The lessons are written as advice to those in the rest of the organisation, to tell them what they should learn from this incident. The corrective actions will address the issues that need to be addressed in the part of the business where the incident happens, while the lesson will help other employees know if they need to take corrective action as well. So the lessons summarise the learning from the incident as recommendations and action points for the rest of the organisation. These are written in the incident report, and then transferred to a shared learning system such as a lessons learned database or a wiki. Case Study 12.1 describes how one organisation transfers lessons from incidents to a corporate wiki.

In some cases it may be that a lesson needs to be applied right away before any report is written. This would be a critical fault or failure that the investigators had found and recognised needed immediate attention or action in other parts of the organisation or industry as whole. Other lessons will be identified during the report creation, and actions assigned.

As we have explored in this chapter, lessons from incidents can only be identified if the investigation process used is thorough enough to identify the basic root causes. From these you can then develop the key findings and hence decide, through consultation, what the lessons will be. Remember that lessons are part of your education process and therefore need to be in a form that can be easily understood and applied. See Chapter 6 for discussion on how to write lessons. A lesson doesn't involve learning if it is not or cannot be applied.

You need a system to ensure that lessons are acted upon. Individuals in the safety functions of the business should be responsible for reviewing lessons from other parts of the business, and for reporting that they have taken action as a result (or if they haven't taken action, reporting why no action is required). All too often companies attempt to create a lessons learned system, but lose sight of the resource required to maintain it, refresh it, keep it current and ensure that where lessons need to be applied and actions taken, then these actions really are taken.

The final report

There are many different styles of producing a final report. I recommend it should have the following structure:

- a summary (easier to be written last once the main report is completed)
- the main body
- background details
- evidence
- analysis of root causes
- corrective actions
- recommended lessons
- a signatures page
- appendices
- facts
- supporting data (drawings, photographs and so on).

Your report should align to the objectives set out for the investigation team, and addresses the incident events and root causes. It identifies how to fix the system by clearly stating the intended actions. These need to be practical, feasible and achievable. They should eliminate or reduce risk. Managers should approve the final report, so having clear actions with recommended closure dates will help them assign the actions to the right individuals.

Case Study 13.1 A simple example of an incident

This is a simple example of an incident, and the root causes, corrective actions and lessons. It should illustrate how these three things are different, but all are steps towards ensuring that the lessons are learned and that the incident never reoccurs.

In this example a nitrogen line was used by a contractor thinking it was an air line. Confusing nitrogen and air is potentially lethal – nitrogen produces an inert atmosphere, with no distinctive smell or colour, which will suffocate anyone who enters that atmosphere. Therefore it is vital to keep nitrogen lines and air lines separate and distinct, and to investigate thoroughly any incident where the two are confused.

The investigation

Usually nitrogen lines have different connector fittings to air lines. Because you should only be able to attach a nitrogen hose to a nitrogen fitting, this was deemed to be an adequate safeguard. Investigation showed that the contractor had removed the unique fitting at the hose station, and the contractor's own air line connector was fitted. It was found that the system wasn't labelled: the label had come off through weather or other damage, and so the contractor didn't know that this was the system employed, and that this was why the connector did not fit.

These corrective actions were decided:

- Check all systems (air and nitrogen) and label them appropriately, with weatherproof labels.
- Educate personnel on the principles of hose management on site.

The principles and processes of safety investigations

The lessons and actions were decided:

- Spread knowledge of the incident through the communities of practice, request feedback on how other sites manage their hoses, and gather consensus of best practice.

- Propose that the company standard be updated so that hose fittings in future will be required to be tack welded in a way that they cannot easily be replaced.

- Propose updating the piping standards, so that different coloured hoses will be used to identify different utilities. This makes it easy to identify hose-to-pipework connections, as pipework at the station will be painted the same colour.

The ultimate safeguard would be to use two different sizes and styles of fitting so that a wrong interconnection can never happen. Therefore the problem would not just be fixed, but eliminated. This lesson should be passed up through the organisation to a level where someone has the authority to make this far-reaching decision.

14

Learning lessons in networks at Mars, Inc

Linda Davies

Linda Davies is the Knowledge Management Director for Mars Information Services. She was the author of the Mars knowledge management strategy, and currently heads a UK-based team responsible for introducing and sustaining knowledge management approaches in the organisation.

Mars, Inc, is a global company in the fast moving consumer goods industry, with six business segments including chocolate, pet care, Wrigley gum and confections, food, drinks and symbioscience. These segments generate total annual revenues of $30 billion. Mars has been a family-owned company for nearly a century; the company is guided by five principles: quality, responsibility, mutuality, efficiency and freedom. The global reach of Mars' business segments and the inclusive nature of these values make it important for Mars to learn, disseminate and apply lessons, while the fast-moving nature of the business makes it difficult to operate a traditional lessons learned approach.

Mars uses the concept of global practice groups (GPGs) to address key strategic challenges. These groups are communities of purpose, [akin to the communities of practice discussed in Chapter 11] – networks of senior associates who are charged with delivering a step-change in performance in an area of strategic importance to Mars, Inc. Each GPG has a sponsor within the Mars Presidents' Group, a leader who directs, mentors, enthuses and enables the network, and a co-ordinator who brokers the connections, provides a base level of resource and generally functions as the 'energiser bunny' of the group. The GPG members comprise senior associates who have responsibility for the overall area in their business units – those who can effect change.

In 2004 the Mars presidents identified a challenge in our newer markets in the developing world. These are markets where the bulk of consumer spending occurs in small local shops and the European–US model of large supermarkets has yet to take hold. We wanted to achieve a step-change in the number of small retail outlets that sell our products, and so drive a rapid increase in sales in these markets. The challenge covered 12 markets, in which there are approximately 12 million shops, and 3.5 billion potential consumers of Mars products.

In order to meet this challenge, we set up the 'Route to Mass Market' GPG, and invited the sales directors of the 12 markets to be the core members of the group. Each of these directors has full responsibility for, and control of, the sales forces in their markets, and full independence in how they operate. In 2004 these markets were at varying stages of evolution. We knew that there was a significant (though varying) amount of lessons and expertise available in 'pockets' around the world, and that each member had unique areas of expertise and real success stories to share. However, no one director held all the lessons, and as the group started to interact it was clear there were critical challenges running as a common thread across the markets. It was like trying to complete a jigsaw in which each person held some of the pieces but no one had them all! At the GPG launch meeting in Munich we agreed the overall picture we were trying to build – since then it has been a matter of finding out who holds which piece of the jigsaw!

The GPG meets every six months, face-to-face, hosted by one of the markets. The meetings are focused on sharing, learning lessons and discussing. There are no formal presentations – numbers and details are covered outside the meetings. Instead the meetings are based around three main activities designed to encourage the GPG to share its lessons and to build the knowledge base of successful processes and principles:

- learning from where we are (learn during)
- learning from what we know (learning from others)
- learning from the last six months (learn after).

Learn from where we are

At a practical level, every market is different. Every market has its own challenges and has innovated and evolved its own solutions. However, at a top-line level the challenges are the same and the essence of what we are trying to achieve is the same. At this level, the basic ideas present in each market contain valuable lessons, which can be adapted and evolved for other markets. This is the essence of learning from the local market, which shares its basic concept with a peer assist via a meeting which combines elements of peer assist and knowledge handover (see Chapter 11). One day of each meeting is spent working with the sales force in the market in which the meeting is being held. The day begins with a briefing on the local market and its structure, including the top three challenges that the business unit is currently facing. The GPG members spend a day working in smaller groups with an experienced local sales associate, looking at a broad range of retail outlets. At the end of the day the GPG reconvenes to give feedback. This happens on two levels.

First, each smaller group provides detailed feedback on what they see as working well in the market – how to build on the successes they see. They also give their top ten ideas on how to address the challenges, based on lessons and experience from their own markets. In this way the host market receives positive confirmation of their success and how to build on it, plus around 30 ideas and improvement suggestions targeted at their key challenges, based on lessons from proven, practical experience elsewhere in the world.

Second, each GPG member nominates the one idea they saw during the day which they plan to adapt and implement in their own home markets. This builds realisation that everyone can learn from every experience, and encourages the rapid adoption of new ideas. More so since each subsequent meeting will follow up on the implementation of these ideas!

Does it work?

Many of our markets have multiple tiny outlets – kiosks at train and bus stations and tiny convenience stores comprising little more than a few square metres of floor space. In these outlets space is at a premium. One market developed a unique way of displaying our products, which made use of previous 'dead' space for the shop owner. When the GPG members went on tour through the market area, the impact of this idea was obvious. There had been rapid uptake by the shop owners, and this new practice became the number one lesson from the GPG meeting. Today you will see the same idea replicated in many of our markets and it is acknowledged as having already delivered huge benefit.

Learn from what we know

This session focuses on sharing an existing area of expertise. Known to the group as a 'show and tell', each meeting contains a three-to-four-hour session focusing on practical examples of solutions to a current hot topic. Before the meeting the group identifies the topic of interest through voting and ranking. It may be a topic where a couple of markets are known to have expertise which the others need; it may be a topic where all have expertise, and where there is interest in seeing the other good ideas; or it may be a topic where it is accepted that a more common approach would be beneficial. Each person at the 'show and tell' meeting has a 'display' in the room to exhibit the solution they are proudest of, and a time slot to 'sell' this solution to the group as a whole. These solutions are always practical; it is a display not a presentation! People are encouraged to bring objects which can be picked up, equipment to trial, or photographs of shop displays. We have even built entire shop displays in hotel boardrooms! These sessions invariably create a huge amount of discussion and it is common for people to leave the meeting with samples of equipment from other markets, to implement themselves when they get back home.

Does it work?

In the June 2008 meeting the 'show and tell' focused on methods of communicating with a dispersed sales force. Many of the emerging markets are huge, with a widespread sales force employed by a third party, who work remotely. The directors therefore may have very limited opportunities to communicate directly with the sales associates.

One particular challenge was how to ensure the sales force have complete clarity about the display and sales targets and focus areas required from them each month. The sales director from Brazil showed a very simple solution they had developed – easy to produce, easy to communicate and, most importantly, easy for the sales force to understand. It generated a significant amount of interest and discussion. In September 2008 during a field visit in Egypt, a salesman was asked about his targets for display materials. In response he explained, clearly and correctly, using the communication he had received – identical in format to the one seen from Brazil. A solution had travelled half the way round the world and been implemented in three months!

Learn from the past six months

Each meeting begins with an update session. These involve only a very few sales metrics, and focus instead on what has worked well and why, how lessons shared at the last meeting have been re-applied, and how the current challenges are evolving. The focus is on learning, talking and discussing, not presenting. In concept it is a mini after action review (see Chapter 5). Each person gets time to talk, each uses the same format, each is expected to discuss both their successes and their challenges. There are three common outcomes that emerge during this session:

- Lessons from one person's success are identified, which are of use and interest to others facing a related challenge. Actions follow, to link those involved either during or after the meeting.
- A common challenge is identified. This becomes the subject of planned learning (such as how best to sell products in open 'wet' markets).
- Successes in a similar area are identified. Actions follow to formalise the learning into a common process.

Not all the answers were known at the start. The whole GPG has been on a journey of exploring and learning. At each meeting, challenges are identified and a decision taken on how to address it. For challenges where no one has the answer, the group as a whole uses its collective experience to brainstorm the options. These are prioritised and individual markets volunteer to test the solutions. These pilot markets test and learn on behalf of the group as a whole. At subsequent meetings they feed back their progress, solutions and lessons. Other markets adapt and adopt these solutions as required, and so join the learning loop.

Does it work?

When the group formed in 2004, getting to the right business model was the first priority. Much of the discussion was focused on the practical elements of the business model in each market. Actions taken were largely around adapting and adopting the mechanisms of developing the retail network. At each meeting, people would share their progress. The sessions became increasingly interactive, with other group members offering advice and suggestions. It has become a highly supportive session and remains a key feature of each meeting. In 2009 all have a robust model delivering profit, and although this is no longer a challenge (thanks to the lessons and solutions shared during the meetings) we believe we can continue to evolve and improve the process by continuing the process of sharing.

Formalising the learning

Practical learning is immensely important for this group and is the focus of their meetings. However, it was also recognised that some level of formal capturing of the lessons was essential, in order to develop a knowledge base. This would:

- bring new starters quickly up to speed
- share the learning of this group with the wider audience in Mars, Inc
- ensure we did not forget what we learned as our expertise developed.

The group identified its key areas of learnings: the topics which had delivered the most value within the GPG, and those which were believed to be of most value to associates in other markets and product sectors. In each of these key areas a programme of formal knowledge capture was established, and the learnings were captured in three formats which support each other:

- a series of booklets containing top tips and advice
- a wiki containing detailed information, templates and examples (see Chapter 10)
- a series of modular training courses.

The booklets and training courses are a valuable source of knowledge for those starting out or starting a new market. The wiki allows the GPG to update its knowledge base as it continues to evolve and learn new lessons. Together they provide a comprehensive guide to winning in the small retail channel.

Summary

Overall there are a number of conclusions we can draw about effective lesson learning in a global network such as this:

- It is important to get the network into a rhythm of learning and knowledge sharing if it is to become second nature to the group.

- Have regular meetings, face-to-face where possible, since the social interactions are key to building the level of trust required.
- Establish the format of the meetings early and keep it consistent so that the core members know what to expect and what is expected of them.
- Keep the meetings focused and relevant to the members so they get real personal benefit from the sharing sessions.
- Keep it practical, so it is obvious to see how to apply what has been learned.
- Always include a session to follow up the learnings taken at the previous meeting. Ask people to say how they have used the lessons and ideas, and what the impact has been. This encourages people to take time to seek out and use the knowledge of others, encourages those who take the time to share their lessons with others and confirms the behaviour we are seeking.
- Celebrate success, and by doing so recognise and reward both lesson seekers and lesson sharers.

And overall for the business – *does it work?* In the five years this network has existed, sales in the small retail channel in the 12 markets have trebled and the percentage profit has more than doubled, adding around $250 million to the bottom line. It would be unfair to claim this was entirely due to knowledge sharing, but the GPG members themselves clearly point to the ideas and lessons they have gained from others as fundamental to their success. I guess you could say it has worked!

15

Wikis as part of a learning system; a conversation with Peter Kemper

Peter Kemper is a leading expert in the use of wikis as a component of a learning approach. He is currently the expertise holder for virtual teamwork for his parent company, a role that includes managing the knowledge management portfolio, researching and innovating in knowledge management, and leading the programme to implement an enterprise-wide wiki encyclopaedia for the whole global organisation. I spoke to Peter in order to understand the role that wiki technology can play in organisational learning.

NM   Peter, can you tell me the history of your involvement with 'learning from experience'?

PK   You have to go back to the mid-1990s for the start of this history. At that time, information management and knowledge management technology was based on simple structures of client servers, but during this time we saw the breakthrough of intranets. On an intranet, you could connect anybody with anything. At the same time, we were beginning to realise that the classical model for learning – of people coming together in classrooms to learn – was no longer sustainable. We had to do more with less, and we had to bring learning to the people, rather than bring people to the learning.

        That combination of new technology and new attitudes to learning resulted in the idea of 'blended learning', where you combine individual nuggets together into a learning package. Some nuggets are delivered through the traditional classroom route, others are delivered through technology.

During this period my organisation was working closely with Betty Collis, Professor of Networked Learning at the University in Twente, Netherlands, and we realised that blended learning could be extended on the informal side. Virtual learning environments were very formal, but we realised that the informal side was equally important. This is where we started working with coaching, mentoring and wikis. The global networks, supported by Q&A technology, were also a core component of informal learning. The power of the network is to provide a means of giving you the answers to operational problems and questions, through access to people in your network that you may not know personally.

The combination of formal training, and informal learning through knowledge management, makes up the whole of the learning space. In learning we focus on people. Technology systems are very important; we are still enabled by technology, but it is still a mistake to put knowledge management as part of the IT department. Many companies that have introduced wikis through the IT department have failed, for example.

NM How has your approach to the use of technology to support learning changed over time?

PK Before the wikis were introduced, we were using knowledge capture systems to support learning from experience (and are still using them). These are transactional systems [structured data held in a database], in combination with document management. The transactional systems hold very structured data, in contrast with the much less structured data in wikis. The computer system maintains the structure. People would write a record, they would put in the metadata, like the date, author and so on, and it is very formalised.

NM What are the issues with transactional systems?

PK The Ford best practice replication (BPR) system [described in Chapter 12], for example, is a combination of a transactional system, and a link to the document management system. You need to fill in the required metadata, and there are some things you cannot escape filling in such as the business unit, the region, the dates and so on. Best practices are identified in the business units, and there are focal points for BPR in the business units.

So a single person has to gather the information from other people, and put it into the system. This is very good in terms of quality control, but you also have to recognise that this focal point acts as a filter, and is often receiving information third hand. BPR has a workflow attached, and each best practice submission is looked at, to say 'could we promote this best practice to regional status? Could we promote it to global status? If it is global, could we tell the assets to implement it?' Within the process there is a validation step, and an expert report can be linked to the best practice as an attachment.

From a process design perspective, this is very robust and fail-proof; however, the risk here is that the workflow can become more important than the content. In some assets, this work is done very well, but the level of insight may vary from oil platform to oil platform or from asset to asset. Regional and global discipline leads are supposed to have the overview of the BPR system, but some of them stepped away from the system and delegated accountability downwards to the process owners, or even to admin staff. The knowledge can often be so fragmented that regional and global discipline leads may no longer be knowledgeable enough to take decisions, so the IT workflow system model fails. The parameter around the decisions cannot be captured in an IT workflow model.

NM What level of success can a transactional system have in spreading global good practices?

PK I have to say one thing here. You might come up with good practice on some specific piece of equipment, but how many versions of that piece of equipment do you have around the world? We don't actually know. Local systems hold information about equipment, but we don't hold any equipment information globally, other than financial information. May be in 10 or 20 years we will have a global overview of technical knowledge about equipment, but any replication system for best practice assumes that there is a global standardisation in equipment, which just does not exist at the moment.

We naturally want to look at things from the overall global perspective, but in fact the real value might be regional and often only local. There might be far more value in replicating and standardising practice around the Gulf of Mexico, for example, where at least the probability of standard equipment will be higher, than trying to replicate and standardise practice globally. Longer term increased global standardisation may change the focus from local to regional to global and the BPR may help to achieve this but the Catch 22 needs to be carefully managed. Important here: it is not a project; it is a journey!

NM So what do you think could provide a better solution than transactional systems?

PK The risk with transactional systems is that they can undermine the creative, tacit side of best practice. If I ask you to share a lesson with me and then confront you with a system to fill in, if the system doesn't fit your situation, then within 30 seconds it annoys you and you become very impatient. That is the downside of transactional systems. If you are in the invoicing department, and have to fill in invoices, then certainly you have to use a transactional system, but as soon as you have got a transactional system applied to the voluntary supply of lessons, it is a bother. In contrast, the ability to be creative is fundamental to Web 2.0 tools such as wikis.

Imagine that one of the fields to fill in is the value of the lesson, which was a required entry in the Ford BPR system. This is very popular with managers, and the discipline heads are particularly interested in the value figures. They feel that this should be a mandatory field. However, it is very difficult to assess the value of the lesson, and the poor guy on the project is putting in the lesson, and maybe he only has five minutes, and here it is asking him to judge what the value is. He will just get annoyed.

With transactional systems, you assume that what is filled in is correct, but there is an example I always think of from the Dutch police. If you have your bicycle stolen, you telephone the police and they fill in a form to record a description of your bicycle. The data show that 99 per cent of stolen bicycles in Holland are ATBs [all terrain bicycles]. This is not true! It is just that most people don't know what sort of bicycle they have; the police have to fill in something, ATB is the first box, and therefore this becomes the default.

There are disadvantages with the document management side of the transactional systems as well. Documents are free in structure, but here we have a constraint of format. If you want to look through one of the documents, the first thing the document management system says is 'you need to check it out'. This is for good reasons of version control, but the poor user thinks, 'check it out? What is going on?' It is counterintuitive for the user.

I believe that the format and nature of transactional systems create a dilemma with the voluntary nature of adding information. That is why wikis came to the surface. The format issues disappear, and the downsides of transactional systems disappear. Some of the information is less detailed, certainly, but you have the lowest possible threshold of entering data. That is the attractiveness of a wiki.

NM   Certainly the barrier to enter information into a wiki is much lower, but are you not raising the barrier for retrieval? Part of the value of transactional systems is that they can be sorted, searched and metricated.

PK   Yes, you are raising the barrier for retrieval compared to a transactional system. However, in a wiki you have a single document which is highly transparent and highly linked, and these advantages can counterbalance what you lose in terms of retrieval. If a wiki is highly used, completely transparent, and is supported by good back office systems, then you are back in balance.

The other advantage is that the wiki should be self-correcting. The moment I classify something wrongly, people all over the company will notice and become alarmed. Whereas the example of the ATB bicycles shows that transactional systems can give you a false assurance in terms of the quality of the data.

I don't want to abandon the transactional system completely, and maybe we can work the other way round, and separate out the *replication* of lessons and best practice from the actual *capture* of the knowledge? But certainly we shouldn't be starting with global replication and standardisation as the main objective.

NM   How would the lessons loop operate in a wiki-based system?

PK   Typically the wiki operates from the bottom up, and there will be no global approach. The angle for introducing content is also different with the wikis than it is with the transactional system. Content comes from learning systems and from incident reports, it doesn't start with 'I want to share this.'

In the past, many lessons from safety incidents may have been put into documents and stored in cupboards, leading to a risk of the lesson not being learned (and thus the incident recurring), as the documents may not be found, may be read out of context, or may be read as part of a wider set of documents which are not consistent. But now we are taking LFIs [lessons from incidents], which are driven by the senior leaders in safety, and putting them into the wiki. We are not replacing the document; we are taking some of the content from the documents and putting it into the wiki, and then we are pointing to the document, for further detail.

The actuality of smaller nuggets of knowledge in a single current, updated and transparent wiki is much higher than in a randomly selected document from the files.

NM   What sort of quality assurance and back office support do you need for your wiki system?

PK   We operate a quality project in the wiki in order to make the right connections.

A document is a silo, and a document in a wiki is also a silo if there are no links. The words in the documents can be linked to equipment, to assets, to processes, to people, but you have to *make* that link. That is what the people in the back office do – they put in the links. If the links are in place, Web 2.0 makes your traditional document management system eight times more used! Documents in a document management system are like documents in a closed cupboard. The wiki opens the doors.

NM   So if lessons can be captured in a wiki, how are they taken forward into action, and improved processes?

PK   Currently there is no route to connect the wikis to the process owners. Maybe now we need to look at the replication steps in addition to the content creation and linkage. There is work to be done, and we are not there yet. However, we do know that we have to have a critical mass of content. Content doesn't come from individual incidents or individual practice, and it has to have critical mass.

NM   Do you have any views on how Web 2.0 technology could help link wikis into a lessons workflow? Perhaps through forwarding new content to people who need to act on it?

Wikis as part of a learning system

PK	You could use tagging. We are currently implementing an open source tool called Scuttle, which is a tagging tool. I used to be dead against tagging, but I am now all for it, and one thing that you can tag is a wiki URL. My role model here is Delicious.com (and there are alternative tools).

RSS feed could be used as well. Wiki technology comes with RSS, and you don't have to convince me that RSS is a winner. At the moment we are using email notification, but it is on my list to get RSS feeds to be as important as email notifications very soon. However, at the moment users can subscribe to words or to word structures and email will deliver you all the notifications you need.

NM	And what about the culture change that needs to go with this, Peter? Have you any ideas on how that could be accomplished?

PK	Connecting local with global knowledge sits not in systems, it sits in behavioural change programmes, and making people connected with each other. But we have to realise that this conflicts with the trends in society. Society is tending towards speed, which means loss of quality. I read recently that one of the UK quality newspapers is at risk of disappearing, and that is because scoop time now is less than an hour, and if you want quality news it takes much longer than this. This is the generation that grew up with calculators; people type in the numbers and just accept the end results without doing the balancing quality check. This search for speed over quality is very deep in behavioural aspects, and systems will not solve the issue.

At the heart of knowledge management is behavioural change, and the connectedness of people, within a society or within a culture.

NM	So how do we ensure quality, in this world of speed?

PK	The issue with wikis has always been, who validates? Our philosophy in my company has been a mix of the wisdom of crowds, the assignment of validation roles, and the use of a back office support resource. Someone with a validation role, someone with discipline authority, an experienced company expert, can validate and edit a wiki very rapidly after it has been updated. This is not just a philosophical question; in an enterprise such as ours you need to have controls in place.

However, a transactional system needs to be validated as well. The story of the ATB bicycles reminds us how easy it is to be fooled. Validation is something you need to think about and constantly work on. The triumph of speed over quality is an overall reality, and we need to retrain people to think for themselves, to validate for themselves, and not just take things at face value.

NM   Peter, thank you very much indeed.

16

How not to learn lessons

In the previous chapters we have looked at how an organisation can learn lessons from the past, and embed them to improve future performance. We have looked at the success factors, the things you have to get right, the processes, the technologies and the accountabilities. In this final chapter, we will turn it around, and look at how *not* to learn lessons. If you follow any of the advice in the list below, you will hinder lesson learning. If you follow all of the advice, you need never learn a lesson again! Here are 100 ways to destroy lesson learning:

1. Learn only from mistakes. Why learn from success? You know you'll never repeat it!
2. Don't schedule your lesson identification, just react to events in an ad hoc manner. That way you can miss many of the key lessons from projects that delivered as expected. After all, nobody minds if progress reporting or budget management is ad hoc, so why would they mind about lesson learning?
3. If you schedule the lesson identification late enough in a project, the project team will have disbanded and you won't have to do it at all.
4. If you do have to schedule lesson identification, then don't use an established process for this, and don't give people any guidance on how to do it. It is much more fun if they have to make it up for themselves.
5. For significant projects involving a large number of people, allow no more than half an hour, once a year, for lesson identification. Any more than this would just mean getting into detail.
6. If the five questions of the after action review are OK for learning from a short task, then they are OK for learning from a complex multimillion-dollar ten-year project as well. Why complicate your learning?

7. If you are holding a lesson identification meeting for a project, and there is a similar project starting up soon, then you need to ensure that nobody from the similar project is invited to the meeting. They would get too excited, and so spoil the atmosphere of calm, disinterested detachment.

8. Ideally, allow people to identify lessons in isolation, rather than discuss them through dialogue or at a meeting. That way you will be sure to stay at the superficial level, and never capture the 'deep lessons'.

9. This will definitely be the case if you give them no guidance or template, just a blank sheet of paper to fill in.

10. Don't involve the whole team in lesson identification. In fact, why involve any of the team? The project manager or team leader can identify the lessons, and that way you can be sure to get a one-sided view of things.

11. Avoid the use of a facilitator for lesson identification meetings. They would only end up challenging the team, and asking awkward questions, which would make it very difficult to avoid getting at the truth.

12. At the lesson identification meeting, allow random conversation. It is much more fun to let conversation wander rather than homing in on specific learning points.

13. If you (as facilitator) have to interject with questions, ask closed questions in order to get minimal answers.

14. Whatever you do, don't ask any questions about what should be done in the future. Stick with talking about the past, it is much safer.

15. Combine your lesson identification processes with personal performance assessment, and assignment of praise and blame. This will really cause people to clam up.

16. Don't base your lesson identification on solid performance data. Why analyse facts, when it is much more fun to collect speculation and opinion?

17. Don't relate your learning review to the original objectives and deliverables of the project. It is more creative to reinvent history.

18. Root cause analysis is just too difficult and too awkward. Stick with the superficial high level things, and you will get your learning over with much more quickly.

19. Don't assign any roles and responsibilities for lesson identification. It is better if everybody thinks it somebody else's job.

How not to learn lessons

20. If you are collecting lessons from an individual, don't brief them in advance. Surprise them, and have fun.
21. Also don't do any preparation yourself, to familiarise yourself with the interviewee; you will find out about them during the interview so why bother to brief yourself beforehand.
22. Don't record the interview. I am sure you can write fast enough to document everything.
23. And if you have to record, don't have a backup recorder, because these things never fail and batteries never go flat.
24. One sheet of A4 paper should be big enough to write notes from a two-hour interview.
25. Let interviewees ramble as much as they like; you can catch up on some sleep.
26. Don't follow up on the interview by requesting additional material; your interviewee may have mentioned some crucial documents but nobody else will want to read them.
27. Evaluations, investigations and assessments should never be systematic or objective, but constructed from ad hoc opinion. I mean, who is going to take any notice of them anyway?
28. Once you have collected the evaluation data, feel free to make value judgements, but avoid learning points at all costs. If team members learn enough from your evaluation to be successful, they may never need evaluations in future and you will be out of a job.
29. Don't separate out unique single lessons; combine all your lessons from one project into a single document. That will make it really hard for people to find them in future.
30. Document your lessons at the back of individual project reports. That way people cannot find them without reading the reports from every single project.
31. And if you can hide them on the library shelf, even better.
32. Make your documented lessons as generic as possible. Aim for motherhood statements. Everybody loves these – they sound so wise, but teach you so little.
33. Use fuzzy phrases like 'do it better' or 'do it earlier' rather than actually giving specific advice. The reader of the lesson will be thoroughly confused.

34. Don't give the lessons any consistent structure; it makes them too easy to follow.
35. Lessons should be supplied devoid of context, making it an exciting intellectual exercise for readers to see whether it applies to them.
36. Unless, of course, it is a very simple lesson that can be explained in a diagram, a photograph, or a few lines of text. In this case, you may want to write a 50-page article.
37. In fact the best way to record lessons is as bullet point phrases. Aim for three words or less. A lesson such as 'Improved contracting process' is so terse and economical, it is almost like a haiku or a Zen koan. Something to meditate on.
38. Alternatively, instead of lessons, why not just write a little history of what happened with no moral, no conclusion, and no learning points? Leave it up to the reader to try to guess what they should do as a result.
39. Even better, just tell a pointless story with no message. People will enjoy listening, and go away none the wiser.
40. When writing your lessons, it is best not to have a particular reader in mind. It may be an engineering lesson, but perhaps an archbishop or a ballet dancer may want to read it one day, so avoid using engineering language, and avoid explaining it in ways that an engineer can follow.
41. In fact, it is best to make your lessons as difficult to follow as possible. If people spent all their time learning from your lessons, you would deprive them of the excitement of having to make the mistakes all over again.
42. Don't write down the name of the originator of the lesson, the date of the event, or the value of the lesson. That would make it far too easy for people to know which lessons were important and recent, and who to go to for more information.
43. If a picture tells 1000 words, then why not just write 1000 words rather than attaching a picture to your lesson?
44. Never under any circumstances set up a system of quality assurance for identified lessons; this would put the 'garbage in garbage out' principle at grave risk.
45. Never assign actions to lessons; it spoils the chance for the organisation to learn the lessons all over again. And again. And

again. Actions just lead to change, change leads to improvement, and improvements threaten our comfortable mediocrity.

46. If there are any actions, they should only ever be of one sort: 'circulate this lesson for information'. Certainly don't require anybody to change anything.
47. You can avoid having to change things if you don't make anybody accountable for the actions.
48. You can postpone change indefinitely if the actions have no closure date.
49. Any actions should be assigned by the most junior person present, especially if they are difficult or contentious actions. This will make them much easier to ignore, and much harder for people to treat them seriously.
50. You can avoid much of the risk of learning if your organisation has no process owners for the major processes. If nobody owns any of the processes, then nobody can change them, and they will stay as inefficient as they have always been.
51. If there are process owners, keep their job description as vague as possible and make sure it includes nothing about updating or improving the processes, as this would give them far too much work to do.
52. Process owners should have no expertise in the topic, should not be members of any community of practice, and should have no technical authority.
53. If you can disengage the process owner from the lesson learning cycle, with any luck he or she will never be notified of the lessons in the first place. Certainly avoid any workflow that might push lessons (and work) their way.
54. See if you can avoid a validation step for lessons. Every suggested change is equally valid, and if you spend enough time on trivia, the important lessons may be lost.
55. Avoid management of change procedures as well. Live dangerously – change your processes on a whim, and hang the consequence.
56. All process documents should be given equal weight. See if people can work out for themselves whether they are a mandatory company standard, or somebody's daft idea.

The Lessons Learned Handbook

57. Much fun can be had in choosing how to document a process or best practice. Simple principles – like giving the reader all of the detail all at once, with no logical structure, context or high level summary, in dense text, with no pictures, audio or video – can create masterpieces of incomprehensibility.

58. Store your process guides and best practices somewhere that the user will not find them. Give them misleading names, and hide them in an obscure branch of the folder structure on a remote file server. After all, everybody likes a game of hide and seek, especially when they are urgently searching for useful lessons.

59. Don't date your documents – let people try and guess which the most recent version is.

60. Don't tell anybody when processes have been updated, this would spoil the surprise.

61. If you have a blog at work, this is a great way of telling people about your holiday, and sharing the latest jokes. It would be far too boring to use it for sharing lessons and process updates.

62. The same is true for newsletters. They should only be used for staff announcements, and pictures from the Christmas party.

63. The training department have got their own budgets and their own staff – let them work out what has changed and what has not. It is not *your* job to make sure that training reflects the most recent lessons.

64. It is best to avoid any review of lessons at the start of a piece of work. Just jump straight in and make it up as you go along. The time you save will be needed later on, for coping with all the repeat mistakes that you will inevitably make.

65. A company lessons database is a complete waste of money. Why spend ten minutes searching a database at your desk, when you could spend a leisurely two hours in the library (and still not find the lessons that you know are there somewhere).

66. If you are forced to invest in a database, then certainly don't spend any time developing a taxonomy. Just file the lessons any way you want. Filing them by the last letter of the project manager's surname is quite an interesting approach.

67. The lessons input form for the database should be just one single text box, to allow the maximum of free form creativity, and to eliminate any opportunities for tiresome sorting and searching.

68. The lessons input form for the database should be as difficult as possible. Give people a long, complex template to fill in. They may well fill the first lesson in, but won't come back to document the second one.
69. Why not eliminate the functionalities for sorting and searching the database?
70. And don't introduce any push functionality, as it would embarrass the process owner to be notified of new lessons.
71. A knowledge library is a very bad idea, making it far too easy for people to find things. In my day we had to search through piles of reports to find everything, why should kids nowadays have it any easier? So no portals please.
72. And no search either, thank you very much.
73. As for wikis, I can see no reason why anybody should be allowed to comment on, or edit, documents, processes or best practices. You lot out there should be applying the processes, not commenting on them, so just get on with your work.
74. Having completely sabotaged the formal lesson learning system, we really don't want people to run any risk of identifying lessons informally. Therefore all attempts at setting up communities of practice should be avoided.
75. Any communities of practice that do exist should not be provided with any way of finding each other, asking questions, storing knowledge, or meeting and discussing anything. Give them the bare minimum of tools.
76. The community leader role should be given to the most autocratic technical expert. He or she can be relied upon to rule the community with an iron fist.
77. Choose communities to cover topics which nobody identifies with. Choose topics which people do rarely, and don't like doing. An income tax return community of practice, for example, will be inactive for most of the year and then spend a couple of weeks complaining and grumbling together.
78. It is best if your communities are very small. Big communities are too useful and contain too much knowledge; 20 people should be your upper limit.

79. If you can disempower your community, so much the better. There is no risk in them sharing lessons with each other, if they are not empowered to use the lessons they find.

80. Try and avoid giving your project staff the opportunity to learn from others at the start of their project. Processes such as peer assist give a project an unfair advantage, and should be discouraged.

81. If, by some mistake, a peer assist is scheduled, then make sure its objectives are unclear, that its focus is on criticism and critique, that it is attended only by managers who are senior enough to be scary, and that you have no facilitator.

82. Similarly avoid giving your project staff the opportunity to pass lessons on to subsequent projects. Processes such as baton passing and knowledge handover are also unfair, giving the subsequent projects a much greater chance of succeeding. Why should they be given an advantage? Why shouldn't they start from a position of ignorance just like the rest of us had to? Failure is good for you.

83. You can eliminate ad hoc learning by careful design of your surroundings. Give people individual offices with doors that can be locked; it gives them a great excuse not to interact.

84. Remove any communal areas. People can drink coffee at their desks, with the door securely shut.

85. Remove any yellow pages, telephone directories, or any other temptation for people to call others and ask for their lessons.

86. Clamp down on any online conversation or social software. People are not paid to talk to each other, they are paid to sit there and work, so make sure they have no distractions.

87. There is a lot you can do to discourage lesson learning with the help of senior management. They can start by making their expectations for lesson learning very unclear. If nobody is clear what they should be doing, then most of the time they will do nothing.

88. You can set the expectation for lesson learning too high, or too low. For example, ask people working on a busy project to spend half an hour every day discussing and identifying lessons. Alternatively, require staff working on your most major projects to identify lessons only at the end of the project, no matter how many years the project may take.

89. Even if senior managers have set expectations, they can undermine these by not taking them seriously. Make sure they allow projects to continue without having done required learning, or allow projects to close without having identified their lessons.

90. Ask senior managers to set priorities that over-rule lesson learning. People will soon realise a retrospect is not valued, if it is consistently postponed to make room for another slide presentation to the chairman's sister.

91. If senior managers are required to take part in any lesson identification meeting or process, ask them to decline.

92. There should be no clear chains of accountability for learning, neither within the business delivery organisation, nor within the supporting functions. This would make it too easy for people to know what to do.

93. Never describe your learning system in simple terms. Don't call it 'learning lessons', call it 'quasi-experiential pedagogy'. Call it 'knowledge gardening'. Call it 'Enterprise 3.5'. Confuse people! They love a good buzzword!

94. If there is a central support team for lesson learning, disband it immediately. If nobody supports learning, it will gradually fade away over time.

95. As well as disbanding the support team, cancel any training for lesson identification and learning processes. We cannot have people who are actually skilled in the technologies and processes, just in case they manage to sneak a lesson through the system.

96. In fact, don't have any training or awareness or roll-out for your learning approach. People will find it harder to get value if they don't understand the complete learning cycle.

97. Don't monitor or measure learning activities. If they are not measured, they cannot be managed, and if people know they are not monitored, they will take short cuts, or avoid learning entirely.

98. Even if you do monitor and measure, then for heaven's sake don't link this to any performance management incentives, or to any rewards for recognition. If people know they can avoid lesson-learning activity with no penalty, they will spend their time doing other things they are actually rewarded for. In fact, why not promote people who get out of trouble through personal heroics, rather than the ones who avoid getting into trouble in the first place by paying careful attention to lessons from the past.

99. Learning metrics need to be kept secret. If senior managers saw them, the people who aren't complying with the learning expectations might get embarrassed.

100. If you want to reward people, then reward them for putting lessons into the lessons database. Pay them for each lesson. That way they will know that lesson learning is not part of normal paid work, but has to be incentivised separately. Also you will swamp the database with poor quality lessons, and when the reward is eventually removed, lesson identification will stop completely.

17

Conclusions

Learning from experience is the most basic of human activities, but we have explored in this book how difficult it can be to scale up from learning as an individual human, to learning as a complex organisation of many humans.

We have learned that lesson identification is something that needs to become routine and proactive. When discussing the various methods of lesson identification, we found that many or most rely on effective questioning, and on identifying the root causes behind events. This was further illustrated in Chapter 13 by Johnny Martin.

We also discussed how lessons can be documented without losing value, and about the need to add context to lessons (often in the form of stories). We have found that lessons must not only be identified, but lead to action, as a lesson is not learned until action is taken and until something changes as a result. We therefore need to distinguish between lessons identified, and lessons learned.

We discussed the types of action that need to be taken, including fixing problems, and writing (or updating) processes and procedures. We found that the role of the process owner is essential. These people need to be accountable for process update, and need to be linked into the learning cycle. Also they need to ensure the processes are well documented for the benefit of the user.

The focus of Chapter 9 was the final step of lessons reuse. Here we looked at the link between lessons learned, pre-project learning and training.

Following our previous discussion of formal vs informal approaches and connect vs collect, we saw a range of technologies, from the formal lessons database, to the less formal wiki. Peter Kemper contrasted some of the issues with these two technologies in Chapter 15.

We also learned that any formal, 'collect' approach to lessons can be usefully combined with a less informal, 'connect' approach based around communities of practice, and the use of dialogue-based processes. This was illustrated in Chapter 14 by Linda Davies of Mars, Inc.

We learned the need for governance in the lessons learned process, and how a governance system can not only provide visible senior management support, but also keep those same managers informed of lesson learning activity through metrics and reporting.

And finally we learned 100 ways in which lesson learning can be stopped or inhibited. This underlines the conclusion that, despite the natural human inclination to learn, there are many potential pitfalls in the path to developing a successful learning organisation.

Index

accountability, 43–5, 133–4
   chains of accountability, 134
actions, 72–82
   assigning, 80–1
   associated with lessons, 73–5
   closing lessons, 82
   escalation, 81–2
   factors in selection of action, 79–80
   six main types of lessons, 75–9
      circulation of lesson, 78–9
      fixing a problem, 76
      further investigation, 76–7
      process documentation, 77
      updating procedures and learning materials, 77–8
after action reviews, 54–8
   attendees, 55
   refinery maintenance exercise case study, 57–8
   scheduling, 54
   structures, 55–8
Ask Anglo, 30

baton passing workshops, 125–6
before action review, 98
blended learning, 31, 167–8
blogs, 96, 115
BP, 10, 30, 34, 45, 48, 64, 70, 83, 92, 96, 110, 112–13, 121–2, 124, 135, 141, 151

communities of practice, 118–23
   asking questions and giving answers, 119
   community knowledge library, 122
   critical mass, 121
   energetic coordinator, 120–1
   level of autonomy, 123
   link with explicit learning loop, 123
   sense of identity, 119–20
   social network, 122–3
   Yellow Pages system, 121–2
community coordinator, 120–1
context of lesson, 70
conversations, 128
corrective actions, 153–5

Den Norske Veritas, 152
doctrine, 19, 97
documentation, 92–4

email distribution list, 96
escalating the action, 81–2, 91–2
   local and company learning loops, 82
evaluations, 65–6

facilitator, 44–5, 79
five whys technique, 152–3
Ford Best Practice Replication system, 28, 96, 168–9
   case study, 137

187

formal collect systems, 28–9
formal connect systems, 30
further investigation actions, 76–7

global practice groups, 159–61
governance in lesson learning, 129–38
   chains of accountability, 134
   corporate expectations, 132–4
   framework, 130–2
   monitoring and measurement, 135–7
   reward and sanction, 138
   supporting organisation, 138
   systems, 135–8

high reliability organisation, 142

incident investigation, 66
individual learning interviews, 59–63
   by telephone, 62–3
   documentation, 62
   interview process, 60
   preparation, 59
   process clarification, 59–60
   questioning structure, 61
   recording, 62
   summaries, 61
informal collect systems, 29
informal connect systems, 30–1
institutionalising learning, 19
interviews, 59
   see also individual learning interviews
interviewing techniques, 147–9
InTouchSupport.com system, 122
investigation process, 143–57
   corrective action and lesson identification, 153–5
      simple example of incident, 156–7
   formal analysis, 146–53
      data investigation, 150
      equipment investigation, 149
      evidence organisation, 151–2
      interview, 147–9
      people investigation, 147
      positioning investigation, 150
   preparation, 143–4
   reporting and subsequent steps, 144–5
investigator's toolkit, 144

knowledge handover, 126–7, 161
knowledge libraries, 111–13, 122
   BP Operations Excellence toolkit, 112–13
   knowledge portals, 111–13
   wikis, 113–15
knowledge management planning, 100
knowledge management team, 45

learning, 2
learning curve, 15
learning cycle, 88–9
learning facilitators, 45
learning histories, 63–5
   process, 64–5
learning loop, 16, 20
lesson documentation, 67–72
   actions from lessons, 72
   attachments, 71
   context, 70
   quality assurance and validation, 71–2
lesson identification, 33–45, 47–66
   after action reviews, 54–8
   application, 33–4
   evaluations and assessments, 65–6
   examples of poor lessons, 37–9
   incident investigation, 66
   individual learning interviews, 59–63
   learning histories, 63–5
   post-project reviews, 47–54
   principles, 34–6

Index

quality lessons, 36–7
questioning process, 41–3
roles and accountabilities, 43–5
self-identification vs lesson identification processes, 39–40
stories and lessons, 39
lesson learning, 1–11, 103–16, 129–38, 159–65, 175–84
   at Mars, 159–65
   case studies, 5–7
   governance of, 129–38
   how not to learn lessons, 175–84
   outcome of, 4–8
   technology to support, 103–16
      knowledge libraries, 111–13
      lesson repositories, 103–11
      publish and search technology, 115–16
      tagging, 116
      wikis, 113–15
   value of, 9–11
lesson learning systems, 3–4, 13–25, 135–8
   closing the learning loop, 20
   monitoring and measurement, 135–7
   reward and sanction, 138
   steps in learning, 16–20
   survey results, 22–5
   terminology, 14–16
   trial and error, 20–2
lesson repositories, 103–11
lesson workflow, 89–90
lessons, 35–9, 105–7
   common structure of, 105–7
   poor lessons, 37–9
   quality lessons, 36–7
lessons learned approaches, 27–31
   blended approach, 31
   formal collect systems, 28–9
   formal connect systems, 30

four quadrants of learning approaches, 28
informal collect systems, 29
informal connect systems, 30–1
lessons learned databases, 103–11
   BP, 110
   common lesson structure, 105–7
   metadata, 108–9
   NASA, 38–9
   picture, 109
   process-based taxonomy, 104–5
   push database, 109–11
LinkedIn, 30

management-of-change process, 78
Mars, 159–65
metadata, 108–9
metrics, 135–6
   activity measurement, 135–6
   compliance measurement, 135
   output measurement, 136

natural learning, 9–10

organisational learning, 2–4

peer assist, 124–5, 161
   case study, 125
peer review, 98
post-project reviews *see* retrospects
practice discussion forum, 96
practice leaders, 86
PRINCE2, 34
problem fixing actions, 76
process ownership, 83–94
   learning cycle, 88–9
   lessons workflow, 89–90
   local vs company process owners, 87
   process documentation, 92–4

process owners, 84–8
  practice leaders, 86
  research and development team, 86
  role of, 87–8
  subject matter experts, 85–6
  technical authorities, 85
  shifting patterns, 87
  validation and escalation, 91–2
process review, 98–101
  before action review, 98
  knowledge management planning, 100
  peer review, 98
  scenario planning, 100–1
  technical limits meeting, 99–100
project management framework, 5
project managers, 43–4
project planning, 45
proprietary software, 96
publish and search technology, 115–16
  blogs, 115
  RSS feeds, 115–16
  search engines, 115

Q&A process, 40
  see also interview
quality assurance, 71–2, 172
questions-based process, 41–3

research and development team, 86
retrospects, 34, 47–54, 73
  large or complex projects, 53
  process, 49–53
    closure, 52–3
    discussion and learning points identification, 51–2
    identify issues, 50–1
    introduction, 49
    project achievements, 50
    project objectives, 49–50

sample, 51–2
recording, 53–4
set-up, 48–9
risk management, 21
root cause analysis, 153–4
RSS feeds, 96, 115–16

safety incident investigations, 141–57
  final report, 155
  investigation process, 143–55
SCAT *see* Systematic Cause Analysis Technique
scenario planning, 100–1
Schiehallion Well Team, 10
Schlumberger, 122
search engines, 115
shared learning systems, 6
SharePoint, 96, 110
Shell, 10
social networks, 30, 122–3
specialist investigator, 45
subject matter experts, 85–6
suppositions, 148
Systematic Cause Analysis Technique, 152

tacit lessons, 117–28
  baton passing workshops, 125–6
  communities of practice, 118–23
  knowledge handover, 126–7
  peer assist, 124–5
  promoting conversation, 128
tagging, 116
team members, 45
technical authorities, 85
technical limit meeting, 99–100
technology to support lesson learning, 103–16
  learning loop, 104
  lessons learned databases, 103–11
TRADOC, 97

training, 97
transactional systems, 29, 168–71
trial and error, 20–2

US Centre for Wildfire Lessons, 15

validation, 71–2, 91–2

Web 2.0, 172–3
wikis, 29, 31, 113–15, 164, 167–74
Wikipedia, 29, 114